A GRIM ALMANAC OF

JACK THE RIPPER'S LONDON

1870–1900

A GRIM ALMANAC OF

JACK THE RIPPER'S LONDON

1870–1900

NEIL R. STOREY

SUTTON PUBLISHING

This book was first published in 2004

This edition first published in 2007 by
Sutton Publishing, an imprint of
NPI Media · Cirencester Road · Chalford
Stroud · Gloucestershire · GL6 8PE

Half-title page: Ludgate Hill from Fleet Street,
  c. 1897.
Title page: Waiting to buy 'trimmings' of meat
  outside one of the larger butchers in the East
  End, *c.* 1888. *(Living London)*

**British Library Cataloguing in
Publication Data**
A catalogue record for this book is available from
the British Library.

ISBN 978-0-7509-4859-3

Typeset in 10.5/12pt Photina.
Typesetting and origination by
Sutton Publishing Limited.
Printed and bound in England.

This book is dedicated
with gratitude and respect
to Stewart P. Evans – 'The Guv'nor'

Detectives of H (Whitechapel) Division 1889. *(Stewart P. Evans)*

CONTENTS

THE ILLUSTRATED POLICE NEWS

LAW COURTS AND WEEKLY RECORD.

No. 1,295.

SATURDAY, DECEMBER 8, 1888.

Price One Penny.

WHITECHAPEL MURDERER'S RECORD. EAST END HORRORS. WHEN WILL THEY CEASE?

OPENING THE DOOR TO ADMIT DEATH! MILLERS COURT DORSET ST. ANOTHER ARREST

MURDER OF A BOY AT HAVANT

ARREST OF THE BOY HUSBAND

A TERRIBLE CASE OF THROAT CUTTING NEAR CREWE.

(Stewart P. Evans)

INTRODUCTION

In the long catalogue of crimes which has been compiled in our modern days there is nothing to be found, perhaps, which has so darkened the horizon of humanity and shadowed the vista of man's better nature as the series of mysterious murders committed in Whitechapel during the latter part of the year 1888. From east to west, from north to south the horror ran throughout the land. Men spoke of it with bated breath, and pale-lipped women shuddered as they read the dreadful details. A lurid pall rested over that densely populated district of London, and people, looking at it afar off, smelt blood. The superstitious said the skies had been of deeper red that autumn, presaging desperate and direful deeds, and aliens of the neighbourhood, filled with strange phantasies brought from foreign shores, whispered that evil spirits were abroad.

> Introduction to the account of the Whitechapel Murders in
> *Famous Crimes* edited by Harold Furniss (1903–4)

By the late nineteenth century Great Britain was riding on the crest of its imperial wave. The industrial revolution had seen the country evolve into *the* world superpower, with an empire so vast it could be truly claimed that the sun would be shining on some part of it whatever the time in England. Because there was more wealth to go around, a new class emerged, the middle class, made up of the likes of managers, clerks and administrators, who were able to afford better living standards and demanded better housing. Property speculators were willing to oblige and very soon whole new areas inhabited by 'upstanding' middle-class folk sprang up across the country. But all was not well; the delineation between the 'haves' and 'have nots' had never been greater. Thousands in the great cities were living in poverty and squalor, none more so than those in the East End of London. Here were the underclass and the marginal, the poverty-stricken, the drink-sodden, the orphans, the criminal types, the immigrants, the unemployed, the revolutionaries, all who could be feared and all who proved again and again that something was rotten in the core of mighty Britain. In the very heart of the greatest empire on earth was to be found the rotten stench of such poverty that it could be equated with the deprivation suffered by those living in the poorest corners of the colonies.

THE NEMESIS OF NEGLECT.

" THERE FLOATS A PHANTOM ON THE SLUM'S FOUL AIR,
    SHAPING, TO EYES WHICH HAVE THE GIFT OF SEEING,
    INTO THE SPECTRE OF THAT LOATHLY LAIR.
        FACE IT—FOR VAIN IS FLEEING!
    RED-HANDED, RUTHLESS, FURTIVE, UNERECT,
    'TIS MURDEROUS CRIME—THE NEMESIS OF NEGLECT!"

Punch, 29 September 1888.

Since the 1870s concern for the situation had been shown in the essential Sunday magazines that were religiously read in the parlours of middle-class households. The names and Christian works of Dr Thomas Barnardo and William Booth of the Salvation Army were known across the country. The appetites of the literate had been whetted, and the expanding number of magazines and journals all wanted their own angle on the 'abyss' that was East London. A few had even ventured to send a reporter into this netherworld and publish the experiences and horrors he witnessed in the next edition.

The generation of 1888 had missed out on the spectacle of public execution, as it was now considered to be a vile and inhuman act, but it did not curb their enthusiasm to *read* about the executions still carried out within prisons in every lurid detail. One of the most widely read periodicals of the late nineteenth century was the *Illustrated Police News*. Begun in the 1860s, it was illustrated with explicit and vicarious line drawings of violent crimes, murders, victims (before and after death), strange deaths, monsters and crime-fighters. Even pictorial magazines aimed at the 'better' homes, such as the *Graphic*, the *Sphere* and the *Illustrated London News,* whose pages had been filled with royal visits, weddings, glorious military campaigns and leading politicians, began to include more frequent depictions of disasters, riots, trials, crimes and criminals. It was almost as if every press pen was poised, trembling in anticipation for something to burst out of the abyss, which it did in August 1888, and the streets and pages of the press were soon running with blood.

On Tuesday 7 August 1888 a body, later identified as that of Martha Tabram, a casual prostitute, was discovered brutally stabbed on the first-floor landing of George Yard buildings, Whitechapel. Despite press coverage and an extensive police investigation, led by Inspector Edmund Reid of Whitechapel CID, her killer was not traced. Almost as the press were giving up on the story, another horrible murder of another 'unfortunate' was discovered on Buck's Row, Whitechapel. This mutilated body was identified as that of Mary Ann Nichols, who was known on the streets where she plied her trade as 'Polly'. The press soon connected this murder with the Tabram killing and frantically sought details of other murders in the area to link with this elusive rampaging maniac, whom they dubbed the 'Whitechapel Fiend'. On Saturday 8 September another body was discovered at the rear of 29 Hanbury Street, Spitalfields. This time the mutilation went far beyond cuts and slashes. The police surgeon's report on the body identified as that of Annie Chapman revealed that some of her internal body parts had been taken away by her killer. The press leapt on this 'latest horror' and the *Illustrated Police News* had another front-page sensation. The case was now well in the public eye and clear action had to be seen to be taken. A team led by Inspector Abberline was despatched from Scotland Yard to lead the investigation 'on the ground'. The locals, dissatisfied with police progress and fearful for the safety of the people of the East End, set up patrols and vigilance committees in attempts to run the killer to ground.

On 27 September 1888 the Central News Agency was sent a letter by someone whose name has become infamous, more evocative, than the 'Whitechapel Fiend'. The name came straight from a street parlance understood by a society familiar with Jack Tar, Slippery Jack, Spring Heel'd Jack – step forward Jack the Ripper. In the early hours of 30 September the public were presented with a 'Double Event', where the murderer was allegedly disturbed in his first act and left poor 'Long Liz' Stride with her throat cut in Dutfield's Yard beside the International Working Men's Educational Club on Berner Street. His blood lust unsated, Jack found his second victim in the space of an hour. Kate Eddowes, yet another casual prostitute, was found in Mitre Square. The wounds inflicted upon her were yet more hideous. The typical cut to the throat had been delivered, but her face had further enigmatic cuts delivered to it and there was extensive abdominal mutilation. At her inquest it was revealed part of her womb and left kidney had been removed by the killer. The media hyperbole was kept boiling with witness accounts and statements from acquaintances given to reporters, lurid broadsheets and revelations of suspects arrested and clues to the identity of Jack the Ripper. The press went into overdrive when none other than George Lusk, chairman of the Whitechapel Vigilance Committee, was sent half a kidney. With it was a bloodstained note purporting to come from the killer himself in which he claimed to have eaten the other half and gave the return address as 'From Hell'.

Early in the morning on the day of the Lord Mayor's Procession, when the eyes of the empire would be on the magnificent spectacle in London, Jack the Ripper left the most diabolical and unprecedented of all his murders to be discovered. In her room at 13 Miller's Court, 26 Dorset Street, Spitalfields, the body of Mary Jane Kelly was discovered. Her body was a mass of human evisceration, the walls splattered like a slaughterhouse; there were even body parts left on a table by her bed. None of the police officers present would ever forget what they saw in Miller's Court that day. The grainy black-and-white image of the scene-of-crime photograph can hardly convey the true horror of the murder and mutilation inflicted by her killer. Poignantly, the resignation of Metropolitan Police Commissioner Sir Charles Warren, the man held by many as directly responsible for the police failure to catch the Jack the Ripper, was also accepted on this day.

The investigation and vigilance patrols continued and more letters were sent to newspapers and the police suggesting ways of tracking the fiend or purporting to come from the killer himself. Public entertainments in theatres and music halls were policed for inflammatory content which may just have sparked off the attacks, and even Queen Victoria voiced her concerns, but Jack the Ripper was never brought to justice. Despite the most diligent research and theorising, the mystery killer who walked abroad upon the streets of Whitechapel in 1888 is no closer to being identified today than he was over 100 years ago. Even the policemen involved with the case at all levels appear to

BLIND-MAN'S BUFF.
(As played by the Police.)
"TURN ROUND THREE TIMES,
AND CATCH WHOM YOU MAY!"

Punch, 22 September 1888.

have had differing ideas on who the suspects were and even the actual number of murders committed by Jack the Ripper. Some suggested as few as four, others argued for well over ten and that he carried on in the years after 1888. Most Ripperologists have settled on the canonical five murders of Nichols, Chapman, Stride, Eddowes and Kelly.

This almanac does not set out to prove or disprove any theory, nor does it set about proffering a new one for the world to contemplate. This *Grim Almanac* examines the wider picture of crime, criminals, life and death in London, especially the East End, between the years 1870 and 1900, the London leading up to, during and in the immediate aftermath, of the Jack the Ripper murders. Come and join me on the mean streets of London and look upon every day within this almanac for tales of 'orrible murder, violent

and tragic ends; meet some of the criminal types, from prostitutes, pimps and garotters to snide pitchers, baby farmers and snuffer gangs. They are complemented with a liberal dash of prisons, punishments, disasters and executions of the time. Other tales tell of those who walked the streets of 'the abyss' trying to earn a few honest coppers with the most unusual and desperate occupations, from tater man to tosher. This book is not for the faint-hearted. If you have the stomach for it (you'll need a strong one), come tread the beat of the brave policemen and learn of the dangers and crimes they had to face when a shadowy serial killer stalked the streets of Whitechapel. If you desire to contemplate the fear of the Autumn of Terror, the crimes and times of the most notorious killer of all time, then read on . . . if you dare!

Neil Storey
2004

JANUARY

Waiting for food parcels in front of Sweetings, Cheapside. As early as 5.30 a.m. poor children and widows would start to queue for the daily handouts of stale bread and cakes. The shop would open at 7 sharp and a man would come out with the dole basket; a policemen would be needed to maintain order in the rush. Many was the household who could not have breakfast until this handout was brought to their table. *(Living London)*

1 JANUARY 1886

The body of Edwin Bartlett was found by his wife Adelaide. The doctor was called and Edwin's father demanded a post-mortem be carried out on his apparently healthy son. It revealed that Edwin had been killed by a large dose of chloroform. The case of the Pimlico Poisoning was to become infamous in the annals of criminal history, and the relationship revealed between Mrs Bartlett and Revd George Dyson scandalised Victorian society. Further gasps were heard as the sexual proclivities of the Bartletts were discussed in court, including such explosive revelations as no fewer than six contraceptive devices found in Edwin Bartlett's trousers and a sexual relations and family planning book at the Bartletts' Claverton Street apartment. Beyond the scandal the bare facts of the case hinged on the administration of chloroform. If such a chemical had been given to Edwin Bartlett by force or deception it would have would left his throat and digestive passages burnt on the way to his stomach; but there was no evidence of this. The chemical was only found in his stomach. With 'no evidence to show how or by whom the chloroform was administered', Adelaide Bartlett was found not guilty. Sir James Paget commented after the verdict, 'Mrs Bartlett was no doubt properly acquitted. But now it is to be hoped that, in the interests of science, she will tell us how she did it!'

Courtroom scene at the trial of Adelaide Bartlett, inset left. The Revd George Dyson is pictured inset right.

2 JANUARY 1880

An inquest was held at Islington Coroner's Court, Holloway Road, concerning the death of Micah Boyce (44) of 87 St James Road, Holloway. Her death, according to her husband John, a journeyman butcher, had occurred after a fall down the stairs with a lamp in her hand. The fluid from the lamp set her clothes alight. Mrs Boyce was taken to the Great Northern Hospital on Chelsea Road; shortly before she died from her burns she stated she had actually been hit on the head with the lamp by her husband. A small incised wound was found on her head which may have been caused by the lamp or a fall. The jury returned the verdict that 'the deceased died from burns, but whether they were accidentally or otherwise inflicted the evidence was insufficient to show'.

3 JANUARY 1899

The execution took place of Johann Schneider (alias Richard Mandelknow), a German baker, convicted of the murder of Conrad Berndt in the bakery on William Street, Hampstead Road. The crime was described at the time as 'atrocious'. It was stated that Mr Ross, the master baker, had taken pity on Schneider and given him a night's refuge. During that night, without warning, Schneider had stunned Berndt, one of the bakers, and thrown his body into the bakehouse oven. It was from there that it was recovered in a charred condition. Schneider then ransacked the premises in search of goods and money. When the benevolent Mr Ross arrived the following morning, he enquired where Berndt was and Schneider said he had gone upstairs for a rest. Schneider then struck Ross on the head and stabbed him in the chest. Luckily the alarm was soon raised and Ross was given first aid, which enabled him to recover from his wounds. Schneider was tried and found guilty of the murder of Berndt. By the time of the execution he was in such a weak and helpless state he had to be carried to the gallows and supported on the trap by warders. A drop of 7ft 6in was allowed. Executioner James Billington was assisted by his eldest son Thomas. Death was recorded as instantaneous.

4 JANUARY 1889

The findings of the inquest held at Guy's Hospital on the body of John Kellard (23) were published. On Christmas Eve 1888 Kellard had joined a group drinking at the Queen's Head in Tanner Street, Bermondsey. It was noted he was 'slightly elevated' when he came in. All agreed to pay 2d into a kitty for drinks and Kellard went round with the hat. He thought there was 2d short and at once charged another in the group named Alexander M'Kie with not having paid his contribution. There was a dispute, the money was checked again and found to be right but Kellard would not admit he had made a mistake and picked a fight with M'Kie, using abusive language and all manner of accusations to goad him. The landlady begged him to stop using bad language and offered to stand him a glass of whatever he liked if he would 'give over the jangling'. Declining her offer, Kellard pulled off his coat and offered to fight M'Kie for 5s a side. M'Kie said he didn't want to go to work with a black eye. Kellard persisted and took the challenge to the street where they put up fists under the railway arch. The punches flew and Kellard fell heavily but got up again. M'Kie warded off a blow and Kellard fell with a heavy thud, striking his head on the kerb. He became insensible and was conveyed to Guy's Hospital in a hansom cab. He did not recover consciousness and died a few days later. His body was found to be covered in bruises and the falls he had suffered had cracked his skull. The coroner's court jury returned a verdict of manslaughter against M'Kie and he was ordered to appear before the next sessions.

5 JANUARY 1880

Charles Surety (29) was executed at Newgate for the murder of the 2-year-old daughter of his girlfriend, Mary Ann Pepper. As public executioner Marwood was about to prepare Surety as he stood on the gallows trap, a letter marked 'OHMS' and 'Immediate' was delivered to the prison governor. Purporting to come from the Home Office, it ordered a reprieve for Surety. One cannot help but wonder what went through the murderer's mind as he awaited his fate on the gallows while the governor and the under sheriff discussed the authenticity of this missive. (It is not recorded how long they took over their deliberations.) They decided it was a forgery and ordered that the execution proceed. It later emerged that the letter was a forgery concocted with no clear motive by a Dr Whiteford, who was sentenced to two months' imprisonment and a fine of £50 for attempting to obstruct the course of justice.

6 JANUARY 1897

Reports appeared of the previous day's execution of Henry Brown (32), a carpenter, at Wandsworth Prison for the murder of his wife. The Browns lived on Linon Road, Clapham. During an almighty family row, Brown went berserk, smashing his wife's skull with a coal hammer and killing her almost instantly. He then turned on his aged mother-in-law with the same weapon, causing her horrific injuries, and finally attempted suicide by stabbing himself in the region of the heart with a shoemaker's knife. He was tried, found guilty and sentenced to death. Brown's mental state was assessed by Dr Nicholson, formerly of Broadmoor Criminal Lunatic Asylum, and Dr Brayn, the present superintendent of the same institution, but their report 'was unfavourable to a reprieve'. The execution was carried out by James Billington; a drop of 7ft 3in was recorded.

7 JANUARY 1886

Richard Dadd, a painter famous for his fairy-tale paintings, died on this day. His old home at 15 Suffolk Street, St James's is now marked by a blue plaque. Few people realise Dadd was actually a killer. Despite studying at the Royal Academy and becoming a competent painter, he earned little money and lived from day to day on a diet of ale and hard-boiled eggs. Dadd became increasingly deluded, believing that he was being called on by divine forces to do battle with the devil. On a trip with his father to Cobham in 1843, he killed the old man with a razor and knife. Ordered to be placed in Bethlem Hospital for the Criminally Insane, known to most as 'Bedlam', Dadd was later moved and became one of the first inmates in the newly built Broadmoor Asylum in Berkshire. It was here he painted some of his best-known works, such as *The Fairy Feller's Master Stroke* and *Contradiction: Oberon and Titania*. He was kept at Broadmoor until he died.

8 JANUARY 1889

Postman Charles Osborne Dunn (28), indicted for stealing a letter containing postal orders to the value of 10s and 5s, and waiter Charles Dowse (33) accused of knowingly receiving the same, appeared at the Old Bailey. Neither could get his story straight. Their incompetence and guilt were so obvious the jury took very little time to return a guilty verdict. Dowse, the receiver, got 18 months and Dunn, the thieving postman, was sent down for five years' penal servitude – stealing from the Royal Mail was a very serious offence.

9 JANUARY 1900

First execution of the twentieth century. Louisa Masset (33) was executed by James Billington at Newgate. Louisa claimed she had handed over some £12 and placed her son Manfred in the care of a Mrs Browning, who had just started a 'children's home' (Browning was almost certainly a baby farmer). Manfred was found later the same day in the ladies' waiting room of platform three on Dalston Junction station wrapped in a black shawl. He had been battered with a brick and suffocated. The shawl was traced to Masset and a witness stated they had seen her on London Bridge station at a time consistent with her committing the crime. Masset said she was in Brighton at the time of the murder and the witness must have been mistaken. The jury decided she was guilty beyond reasonable doubt and she was sentenced to death. It is said that as the hour of execution approached, Louisa agreed her sentence was just, but it could be argued this was not a confession to the murder but the concurrence of a penitent mother who had unwittingly sent her beloved son to his doom.

10 JANUARY 1888

An inquest was held at Coroner's Court, High Street, Borough, on the death of Fanny Alden (69), a widow and a member of the sect known as the Peculiar People, whose headquarters were on Bath Street, London Road. A large number of her brethren were present in court and one of their number, Eliza South, gave evidence. She stated that Mrs Alden's health had declined for about seven weeks before her death. The coroner enquired if she had sought medical aid to which South replied, 'We only did what we consider necessary according to our belief. She had laying on of hands by the elders and we gave her all the nourishment we could.' Dr Jones, who had conducted the post-mortem, stated death had been due to serious apoplexy but noted the body was very thin, seriously ulcerated and showed old pleurisy. In summing up, the coroner castigated the sect for their neglect of Mrs Alden and threatened that if the case had been stronger he would have sent it to the criminal court. The jury returned a verdict in accordance with the medical evidence. After the verdict was passed, Elder Brooks was brought before the coroner but he would not accept the warning and stated they would continue to do as they had done; the jury cried, 'Scandalous!' As Brooks attempted to lecture the court on his beliefs, the coroner declined to listen, stating that, 'the ways of these people were quite peculiar enough for me'.

11 JANUARY 1888

James Ostler, a chemist's assistant, who ran and lived on the premises of A.J. Brown's chemist at 55 Trafalgar Road, East Greenwich, walked into the kitchen to discover his 2-year-old son lying on the floor, with his wife Louisa (23), the boy's mother, standing over him; the boy's head had been severed from his body. James asked, 'What have you done?' She replied, 'My Jim; I've only one life to take.' Ostler sent his wife upstairs and sent a neighbour to summon the police. Mrs Ostler was heavily pregnant and had been suffering from increasingly severe religious delusions. Before she was arrested, her sister asked her why she had committed such an act; she replied she had a command from God to offer a sacrifice so that the whole world should be redeemed. Inspector Lander of Park Row Station soon arrived, followed by Dr M'Gavin, who, upon entering the shop, saw Ostler serving a customer. Seeing the surgeon Ostler shouted, 'My wife's insane and has killed my child.' (Note that this horrible slaying did not stop Ostler from attending to his customers.) When attended by the doctor, Mrs Ostler said, 'The child has two natures; one is a human nature, and the other is a beast's nature. The beast's nature must be cut out.' Removed to the workhouse infirmary, she was found to be 'of unsound mind' and committed to the asylum.

12 JANUARY 1889

An article in the *Pall Mall Gazette* names a George Hutchinson as a potential Ripper suspect. Hutchinson, a resident in a lunatic asylum in Elgin, Illinois, had escaped and

"I COULD SWEAR TO THE MAN ANYWHERE" HUTCHINSON.

killed a woman in Chicago. The mutilations he inflicted were said to be very similar to those inflicted on the Ripper victims. He was recaptured but escaped again in 1884 or 1885. Curiously, another George Hutchinson was acquainted with Mary Kelly before her murder but did not come forward until after her inquest, claiming he was not aware of the murder. (This explanation stretches credulity because the streets of the East End, packed with people for the Lord Mayor's procession, were alive with stories of this, the latest and most horrible of all the Ripper murders.) His statement seemed contrived, and his detailed description

George Hutchinson (in doorway) and an artist's impression of the man he saw with Mary Kelly on the night of the murder – was this really the best description we have of Jack the Ripper? (*Stewart P. Evans*)

of the last man seen with Mary has passed down the generations of Ripperologists as one of the best; perhaps it was too good. Some modern Ripper authors suggest that it could just as easily been Hutchinson that was the Ripper and that his description of the man was an attempt to deflect attention away from himself.

13 JANUARY 1885

Horace Robert Jay (23) was executed at Wandsworth for the murder of his fiancée, Florence Julia Kemp (18). Jay and Kemp had been 'walking out' together for some time, but it appears Jay was becoming increasingly protective and jealous of his future wife. After a number of arguments, Jay appeared to have settled down and Florence was happy to accompany him back to his lodgings in Clapham to select apartments in view of their impending marriage. While she was there screams were heard and concerned neighbours who shared the dwelling stormed into Jay's room to find him in the act of cutting Florence's throat with a razor; he then slashed his own. Both were removed to St Thomas's Hospital but only Jay survived. Despite an energetic defence put up by Charles Matthews, who argued his client was not mentally responsible for his actions, Jay was found guilty and sentenced to death. Executioners hate any damage to the necks of their customers and great care was taken by Berry over the drop (lest the head be torn off). A drop of just over 7ft was given and death was instantaneous by dislocation, but the wound was reopened although reports were quick to point out that 'there seemed very little blood'.

14 JANUARY 1892

This day saw the death of Prince Albert Victor, Duke of Clarence (right), eldest son of the Prince of Wales (later King Edward VII), eldest grandson of Queen Victoria and thus second in the line of succession to the throne of England. Known to the Royal family as 'Eddy', he was widely nicknamed below stairs as 'Collar and Cuffs', because of his dandyism. It has also been suggested that the young prince occasionally enjoyed a walk on the wild side of the East End. Eddy became one of the more modern suspects involved with the Jack the Ripper crimes. It has since been proved beyond doubt that the Prince was in Yorkshire, Scotland and Sandringham at the time of the Ripper killings. Unfortunately, the Prince was not so innocent of complicity in the 'Cleveland Street Scandal' in 1889 (see 6 July, p. 103). Prince Eddy was just 28 years old when he died of pneumonia at Sandringham.

People of the Streets: Tater Men

Baked potato sellers or 'tater men', with their distinctive call of 'nice floury taters', would normally be found near pubs and 'four ale bars' (where beer was only fourpence a quart). They would sell baked 'taters heavily dusted with salt' (and a dab of yellow grease they euphemistically called 'butter') to those building up a thirst or leaving the hostelries. Two sizes were offered, 'tops' (large penny spuds) and 'middles' (smaller halfpenny ones); hot potatoes were often the only supper a poor family could afford. The machinery of the trade, a baking oven often formed from an iron baking box with a chimney and looking not dissimilar to a steam engine, was simple and easily pushed as a handcart or pulled by a donkey. Their pitches, like those of many street sellers, would often have been handed down from generation to generation. Any interlopers would soon be met with shouts and, if necessary, fists and stall-wrecking from others in the established street-trading community in the area, the idea being that if someone attempted to usurp a pitch, the other traders would do the same to them.

16 JANUARY 1888

The Revd George Bancroft Butterfield was arrested in South Kensington for begging and being drunk. After he was taken into custody, a number of begging letters were found in his possession. He appeared in court in the same shabby cassock he had been arrested in and apparently suffering from the effects of drink. It appeared that the reverend had once held a good appointment at Mossley near Manchester but had 'lost his position'. Comment was made that Butterfield had 'ill-treated his wife' and she was now 'reduced to earning a living by charring'. The inebriated fallen cleric was sentenced to the house of detention for a week.

17 JANUARY 1889

An inquest was held at Marylebone Mortuary into the death of Charles Dubery Foskett. The young man had been brought home in an insensible condition suffering from injuries to the head and shoulders that were allegedly caused by a horse and cart running over him. Despite recovering consciousness before he died he could not explain how the accident happened. Dr O'Brien was called to the inquiry and stated he knew the family, who had 'the peculiarity that if any one of them received the slightest scratch he would almost bleed to death'. The doctor stated he had known as many as three of the family to be laid out apparently dead at one time, but who were found only to be exhausted through loss of blood. A verdict of 'accidental death' was returned. (The 'peculiarity' suffered by the Foskett family would be recognised by later medical authorities as haemophilia.)

18 JANUARY 1888

Fire broke out shortly after 3 a.m. at the Duke of York Tavern, Ormond Yard, on York Street, Jermyn Street, Piccadilly. Living above the pub was Mr Dale, his wife, a niece and

A handy hansom allows a brave policeman to rescue those trapped in the fire at the Duke of York Tavern. *(Stewart P. Evans)*

the pub potman. Awoken by the crackling and burning of the fire, they all left their rooms and descended the stairs to escape but found the exits blocked by smoke and fire. Only able to reach their upstairs drawing room and having no means of getting down the final storey, they opened the windows and shouted for help. Fortunately, in the nick of time, the quick-witted driver of an empty hansom cab ran his cab alongside the flaming building. A brave policeman clambered up and effected the rescue of the trapped people, to the cheers and applause of the gathering crowd.

Visiting day at Holloway Prison, *c.* 1890.

20 JANUARY Prisons and Punishments: Holloway

Holloway Prison was opened in 1852. Built along the lines of a medieval fortress and complete with battlements, towers and heraldic beast statuary, its original foundation stone bore the legend 'MAY GOD PRESERVE THE CITY OF LONDON AND MAKE THIS PLACE A TERROR TO EVIL DOERS'. Prison staff were expected to maintain high standards of smartness and were instructed to 'conduct themselves calmly'. There were also a series of fines for warder misdemeanours including 1*s* for failing to lock a cell door, 1*s* for wrangling on duty and 6*d* for falling asleep in chapel! It is hardly surprising that no prisoner escaped from Holloway during the nineteenth century. In its early years Holloway had separate wings for male and female prisoners, but between 1892 and 1902 Holloway held only males. In 1902 the situation was totally reversed and it became an all-female prison. The old Holloway was gradually demolished and replaced with a modern women's prison during the 1970s.

20 JANUARY 1888

Conclusion of the trial of Léon Serné (38) and John Henry Goldfinch (30) at the Old Bailey. Serné and Goldfinch worked together as barber and barber's assistant at their premises at 274 Strand. Serné was in financial difficulties and decided the best way to get himself out of them was to insure his property and furniture for £800 and set it alight with newspaper and paraffin-fuelled fires. It was not clear if he intended to get rid of his family too or if they were 'primed' to 'escape' from the fired building. Serné was soon apprehended and he implicated his assistant, Goldfinch. The jury found no clear evidence to implicate Goldfinch, whereas Serné was sent down for twenty years penal servitude. As Serné was taken down, he called out, 'Good-bye friends; take care of my dear wife.'

21 JANUARY 1888

Thomas Nuttall appeared before Middlesex Sessions on an indictment for inflicting grievous bodily harm on PC Harris 185D while he was in the execution of his duty. Harris had been rushing to assist PC Noble, who was being knocked about by a 'rough' on Gee Street, Marylebone. When Harris was attempting to arrest the 'rough', Nuttall came over and struck him a severe blow across the face with a poker, cutting the side of the constable's head, splitting his nose and rendering him unfit for work for the following three weeks. PC Noble blew his whistle, summoning constables and a police sergeant, who came running with truncheons drawn and beat Nuttall to the ground, his fists flying and legs kicking all the way. The full extent of Nuttall's injuries are not recorded, but when he was found guilty the magistrate gave a him the uncommonly lenient sentence of four months with hard labour for his crimes, 'the judge taking into consideration the punishment he had received at the hands of the police'.

22 JANUARY Life and Death in the Abyss: The Brothel

Before the Criminal Law Amendment Act of 1885 that criminalised brothel-keeping, dens of iniquity to suit all classes were to be found all across London. The *Lancet* estimated in 1857 that one house in every sixty in London was a brothel and one woman in sixteen a prostitute. If this is to be believed, it means there were 6,000 brothels and 80,000 working girls in London during the mid-nineteenth century. The cheapest and the worst brothels were to be found in the East End. William Acton, in *Prostitution Considered in Its Moral, Social and Sanitary Aspects*, said this of an 'example' he considered representative of the East End: 'It was kept by a dark, swarthy, crisp-haired Jewess, half Creole in appearance, who stated she was a widow, and having married a Christian was discarded by her own people. . . . We went upstairs and saw the rooms, eight in number, which were let out to as many women. The landlady told us they pay 2s when they bring home a visitor, and she thought that on average they were lucky when they bring two each in the course of an evening . . . . The utmost pressure put upon them is, perhaps, that they are induced to go out and persevere in prostitution when otherwise indisposed to do so.' Prostitutes were all ages, and some 'painted and haggard' women were well into their forties and fifties. In 1888 the age of consent was 13, but in Hanbury Street, Whitechapel, the Salvation Army took in many girls aged between 11 and 12, and some were as young as 10. After the 1885 Act a number of the brothels in the East End were shut down, but in 1888 there were still about sixty-two brothels known to the police beat men of H Division, Whitechapel. As a result of the Act, more girls than ever were caused to walk the streets for trade.

23 JANUARY 1888

James Kelly escapes from Broadmoor Criminal Lunatic Asylum. Kelly had stabbed his wife in the course of an argument in June 1883. He was sentenced to death for her murder but reprieved after questions were raised about his sanity. It has been suggested that the argument Kelly had with his wife was over Mary Kelly, with whom he was having an affair, and that he returned to London, found out she was a prostitute and carried out the Whitechapel killings on those who crossed his path while he was tracking her down.

24 JANUARY 1885

Fenian bombs exploded in some of the most significant and historic buildings of London. A device exploded at the Tower of London, creating havoc in the Old Banqueting Hall. A second bomb was discovered on the steps going down to St Stephen's Crypt in the Palace of Westminister and was reported to PCs Cole and Cox of A (Whitehall) Division. Lifting the parcel with its burning envelope, PC William Cole carried the device up the stairs into Westminster Hall, where his hands were so badly burnt he was caused to drop the bomb and it exploded. Bravely tended by PC Cox, who was on duty in the hall, Cole was later awarded the Albert Medal for his gallantry. A third bomb was detonated in the House of Commons. Luckily the House was not in session at the time but extensive damage was caused to the Division Hall, Strangers and Peers galleries. Two men were convicted of complicity in the bombings and were sentenced to penal servitude for life.

25 JANUARY 1885

Death on Highgate Ponds. There had been a cold snap in the capital and people were venturing on to ice-covered ponds to slide and skate. On this day brave Thomas Simpson (45) labourer, lost his life while attempting to rescue skaters who had fallen through the ice on Highgate ponds. Two other inquests were held on the same day as Simpson's, all deaths through accidents during sliding or skating on thin ice. Edward James Banks (12), son of a watchman of 6 Spencer Street, Dartmouth Park, had fallen through ice while sliding with friends on the frozen Highgate No. 2 ponds. Filled with youthful bravado he had ventured nearer the centre of the frozen pond than anyone else. The ice gave way and he plunged into the freezing waters. Despite efforts by his young friends and John Smith, the gardener who rushed over to help, the boy's body was not recovered until evening time. Francis Annett (30) of Holloway had been skating the day before the death of Simpson and fallen through the ice. He was pulled out by his companions assisted by a passing constable (PC Howard) but remained insensible despite attempts at resuscitation,

26 JANUARY Prisons and Punishments: Newgate

The most infamous of the London prisons was Newgate. It had acquired its notoriety over almost 900 years, not only for its harsh regime, overcrowding and unsanitary conditions, but because it was from here that generations of felons, both the infamous and obscure, were carted to Tyburn for execution. Indeed the infamous 'Newgate Calendar' of executions became the standard reference work to find *the* most notorious criminals who had been brought to justice in England. When the congestion caused by thousands crowding around to observe executions at Tyburn became too much of a headache in 1783, public executions were moved to the open area directly in front of Newgate, where a high portable gallows or 'new drop' that afforded a view of the proceedings for all would be wheeled into place for the ultimate letter of the law to be enacted. The prison known to Victorians as Newgate was the fourth and largest house of detention to be built on the site. Constructed in the 1770s with a conveniently situated Sessions House next door, the high solid walls and massive scale of the prison were deliberately designed to inspire fear of the law and imply that no matter what the crime 'we 'ave room for you in 'ere'. After 1868, when public hangings were abolished

Newgate Prison, *c.* 1895.

and removed to 'behind prison walls', Newgate became the main place for execution in London. Executions were carried out in the shed beside the prison yard, and the crowd outside were notified of the enactment of the sentence by a tolling bell (until 1890), the hoisting of a black flag and the posting of notices on the prison doors. The 'Newgate Hangman' was also the main executioner for London and the man most likely to be hired in by provincial counties to carry out their executions. The job was carried out between 1829 and 1874 by William Calcraft. Newgate finally closed in 1902 and was demolished. The Central Criminal Court in the Old Bailey now stands on the site.

27 JANUARY 1888

Death of George Godwin (1815–88). Godwin wrote two volumes on the churches of London, but his greatest works, *London Shadows* (1854) and *Another Blow for Life* (1864), exposed the deplorable sanitary condition of the capital and its impact on the life expectancy of the poorest members of society.

28 JANUARY 1888 Prisons and Punishments: The Police

Under the Metropolitan Police Act 1829 seventeen police divisions were created with a jurisdiction covering a seven-mile radius from Charing Cross; by 1888 another four divisions had been added. Each Police Division was designated by a letter; in 1888 they were:

Superintendent Thomas Arnold with some officers and men of H (Whitechapel) Division pictured at the rear of Leman Street Station, *c.* 1888. (*Metropolitan Police*)

A – Whitehall, B – Chelsea, C – St James's, D – Marylebone, E – Holborn, F – Paddington, G – Finsbury, H – Whitechapel, J – Bethnal Green, K – Bow, L – Lambeth, M – Southwark, N – Islington, P – Camberwell, R – Greenwich, S – Hampstead, T – Hammersmith, V – Wandsworth, W – Clapham, X – Kilburn, Y – Highgate. There was also CO for Commissioners Office, Railway Police, Thames Division or Dockyard Police at Woolwich and River Police. The square mile of the City of London had its own force known as the City Police. Each constable wore his division designation letter by his numbers on his collar and above his numbers on his helmet plate as a means of identification. The combined City and Metropolitan police forces of London numbered about 15,000 personnel. H Division, Whitechapel, had its police station on Leman Street with Thomas Arnold as superintendent; with him were 38 inspectors, 56 sergeants and 522 constables.

METROPOLITAN POLICE

H DIVISION (WHITECHAPEL)

Fixed Points for Police Constables 9p.m. to 1a.m

Junction of Ben Jonson-rd and White Horse-st, Stepney

Junction of Brick-la and Bethnal-green-rd

End of Christian–st and Commercial-rd,

Church-st. Wapping

Columbia-rd, Bethnal Gn, corner of Hassard-st.

Commercial-rd-east, corner of Bromehead-st.

Commercial-st, Spitalfields, corner of Thrawl-st

End of Flower and Dean-st and Brick-la, Spitalfields

End of George Yard, High Street, Whitechapel

Front of G.E. Rly., High-st, Shoreditch

Opposite end of Great Garden-st and Whitechapel- rd.

Hanbury-st corner of Deal-st, Mile End New Town

End of Hare-alley, High-st, Shoreditch

Hermitage-br, Wapping

Junction of Leman-st, Commercial-st and High-st, Whitechapel

New Gravel-la-br, London Docks (3p.m-7a.m)

Old Gravel-la-br, London Docks (3p.m – 7a.m.)

South end of Ship-alley & St. George's-st-east

Shoreditch Church

Corner of Spencer-st and Watney-st, St George's East

Spitalfields Church

Stepney Rly. Stn, Commercial-rd-ea.

Upper East Smithfield, principal entrance London Docks

Corner of Warner-pl and Hackney-rd

Opposite Sailor's Home Wells-st, Whitechapel

Whitechapel Church

Junction of White Horse-la and Mile End-rd

In the event of any person blasting on a whistle, springing a rattle, or persistently ringing a bell in the street or in an area, the police will at once proceed to the spot and render assistance.

Fixed points notice for H Division, *c.* 1888.

Sir William Withey Gull. *(Stewart P. Evans)*

29 JANUARY 1890

The death of Sir William Withey Gull (73). Gull was raised to prominence after his successful treatment of the Prince of Wales for typhoid fever in 1871 (see 27 February, p. 40). Queen Victoria was so grateful she granted Gull a baronetcy and appointed him Physician Extraordinary to the Queen. Despite being in his seventies and having suffered a stroke at the time of the Ripper murders, Gull was included by Stephen Knight in his Royal and Masonic conspiracy theory of Jack the Ripper. This noble surgeon's name has also been dragged through the dirt on television and in film documentaries depicting him as Jack the Ripper. Sir William died peacefully after a third stoke and was buried at Thorpe le Soken, the small Essex town where he was born in 1816.

30 JANUARY 1890

Reports published of Anne Sanderson (31), who appeared at Thames Police Court charged with having 'taken possession' of a 5-year-old boy while he was on an errand the previous Monday evening. On the Tuesday she took his boots away and left him on a bench to beg at Fenchurch Street station. The little lad fell asleep and was taken to the police station. Sanderson had the gall to turn up at the police station with the boy's boots in her basket, stating, 'I have lost a little boy.' She was taken into custody and it soon emerged that Sanderson had whipped the child to make him call her mother. She was sentenced to three months' hard labour.

30 JANUARY 1888

Albert Martin (52), baker, was convicted at the Central Criminal Court of assaulting PC Charles Adams in the doorway of a house in St Peter's Street, Mile End. Martin had been discovered with another man in the act of attempting to gain entry to the property; when the constable approached, Martin struggled with the officer. The other man struck Adams on the neck. Adams released Martin to arrest the second man, whereupon Martin knocked him unconscious. Martin was arrested a month later on a separate charge and recognised by Adams, who found a chisel on him that matched the marks left on the Mile End door. He stood trial and was found guilty, and it was revealed that he had a string of convictions back to 1864. He was sentenced to fifteen years' penal servitude.

FEBRUARY

Cat's-meat seller, *c.* 1888. Wheeling his barra' on his regular round the cat's-meat man would be hawking slices of horse meat about 4 inches square, five chunks to a wooden skewer, for one penny. He would also be consulted should the cat's owner be too poor to afford the services of a vet and, since he was usually equipped with a herbal panacea, this could be a lucrative sideline. So too was his sale of 'cheap meat, no questions asked' to those too poor to be too discerning.

1 February 1878

Death of George Cruikshank the caricaturist, who was respected for his keen eye for the authentic detail of social suffering and life in the lower orders in his illustrations for Dickens. His satirical cartoons were feared for their frankness and concise conveyance of their topic. One of his earliest works was a satire on a Bank of England note. Hearing of the death sentence being passed on two women found guilty of passing £1 notes, Cruikshank published his own version of a note with hanged bodies, skulls and funereal impedimenta depicted on it. This, combined, with the groundswell of opinion against the unjustness of the sentence caused it to be commuted to flogging and transportation to Australia.

2 February 1898

The police draw a blank in their investigation into the murder of Thomas Webb at West Cottage, College Farm, North Finchley. Webb was the head dairyman of the Express Dairy Company; when standing outside his home on 29 January he was fatally shot. His murderer was never caught.

3 February 1888

An inquest was held by Wynne E. Baxter at the London Hospital into the deaths of Abraham Potzdaner (25), a boot finisher, and his wife Hannah (20). Giving evidence, Louis Cohen stated that when the couple came to England, they lived with Cohen's sister, who kept a cook shop in Brick Lane, and he arranged employment for Mr Potzdaner with his brother. Potzdaner left after just eight days, stating the work was too hard. The deceased woman then came to live with Cohen at 147 Backchurch Lane, Whitechapel, and had stayed for the last three months. Cohen said he had encountered Mr Potzdaner on several subsequent occasions and they had not quarrelled. On the Wednesday preceding the inquest Mrs Potzdaner had left the house on an errand. Hearing screams in the street, Cohen rushed out to find her lying on the road with her throat cut. With her last gasps she indicated the direction in which her assailant had fled and Cohen gave chase, but did not see the estranged husband. PC Collinson 6HR was in Greenfield Street when he saw Mr Potzdaner being pursued by a crowd. On seeing the policeman Potzdaner drew his shoemaker's knife, cut his own throat and stuck his fingers in the gash to open the wound. PC Collinson restrained him in this act and attempted to remove him to hospital but Potzdaner died on the way.

4 February 1896

William James Morgan (56) was executed at Wandsworth. Morgan, a Deptford hawker, had been living apart from his wife for some time when they met up on the street. Morgan asked her to return, she said no and a quarrel ensued in which she threatened to set her son on Morgan if he didn't leave her alone. Seized by blind fury, Morgan took out his knife and stabbed her to death. After his conviction Morgan filled his prison time with prayer, playing cards and deciding which friends he would bequeath his magnificent rowing trophies to. A champion sculler in his day he had even been presented cups by William Gladstone. Morgan was executed by public executioner James Billington assisted by William Warbrick.

5 FEBRUARY 1889

Thomas Barry appeared before the Central Criminal Court to answer an indictment for common nuisance. At his premises at 106 and 107 Whitechapel Road he had mounted gaudy theatrical entertainment hoardings and exhibited such feasts for the eye as a fat Frenchwoman, a female pugilist, a woman described as being half human and half gorilla, and a midget. What had caused particular consternation was the addition in the autumn of 1888 of 'waxwork effigies of the women who were murdered in Whitechapel'. The account goes on: 'A picture was also put on show . . . considered by the public to be too strong, and the people threatened to tear it down.' It is also recorded that an effigy of Jack the Ripper was also added to the exhibition. (I wonder how they decided what he looked like?) The crowds that assembled outside the exhibition and to see the posters and listen to the showman, who would occasionally bark out the entertainments therein, frequently spilled on to the highway and the verdict of the court was that this was a public nuisance. Barry was ordered to enter into his own recognisance and was bound over for the sum of £100.

Punch, 13 October 1888.

6 FEBRUARY 1888

Mary Ann Minty, a destitute widow of Whitechapel, appeared at Lambeth Police Court charged with begging on Walworth Road. She had been found standing in the gutter with her children aged 7 and 10 by the mendicity officer, Joseph Bosley. He approached the pathetic group and explained to them it was probably best that they came with him to the police station. Widow Minty became loud and abusive but Bosley insisted she should go and escorted them to the station. A group of 'roughs' had assembled at the scene and followed, shouting abuse and throwing stones at Bosley. Once at the station the children were given a bath; they were discovered to be covered in vermin which in some places had eaten into their flesh. The court decided 'it was monstrous the mother had deliberately dragged the children about the streets in order to incite the sympathy of those who were stupid enough to believe they were acting in a charitable manner'. Mary Minty was sentenced to one month's hard labour and her children were removed to the workhouse.

7 FEBRUARY 1888

Mary Frances George (50) was indicted for maliciously throwing corrosive fluid over Eliza Maria Wilson. George's husband had left her for Wilson in December, but George could not stand the thought of her husband with another woman. She stormed round to Wilson's house and barged in. On finding her husband and Miss Wilson sitting together, she threw sulphuric acid over them both. The husband was badly burnt about the face and upper body, while Miss Wilson's back was badly burnt. Mrs George was found guilty but mercy was recommended on the grounds of provocation; she was sentenced to twelve months 'with such Hard Labour as she was fit for'.

8 FEBRUARY 1886

The 'Black Monday' riot in Trafalgar Square. Two rival radical movements, the London United Workmen's Committee and H.F. Hyndman's pro-revolution Social Democratic Federation, both made it known they wanted to hold rallies in Trafalgar Square on this day; neither would back out and a violent clash was almost inevitable. Henry Matthews, the new Home Secretary, was preoccupied with getting a grip on the reins of his new office and approved both meetings. A force of constables was designated to police the square with 563 reserves standing by. The meetings in the square went without incident, but as the mob, fired up by the speeches, streamed along Pall Mall, a garbled message was sent to the police that there was trouble in the *Mall* rather than the *Pall Mall*. The reserves rushed to defend Buckingham Palace and the mob was left to run amok in Pall Mall and St James's. An unofficial rally in Hyde Park saw the mob whipped into a frenzy of window smashing and looting along Oxford Street. Inspector James Cuthbert was routinely parading his sergeant and constables ready for their duties when he heard the mob. His actions were swift, brave and decisive. He marched his men, seventeen in number, to Oxford Street and with truncheons drawn they charged the crowd and ended the riot. Two days later a further panic of a large mob assembling to attack Oxford Street saw businesses barricaded and fearing for the worst. However, the mob never came and was probably only ever a paranoid overreaction by police officials on unreliable information. An inquiry was held into the incidents and Metropolitan Police Commissioner Henderson took the only option open to him and resigned. A man with a strong military background was needed to head the police and deal decisively with such incidents, so he was replaced by General Sir Charles Warren.

9 FEBRUARY 1888

Reports appeared of the inquest held by Mr Langham, City Coroner, on the body of Henry J.S. Agnew (39) of 32 Granby Street, Hampstead Road. The evidence presented revealed that two years previously the deceased had been violently attacked by two ruffians as they attempted to rob him as he returned home late one night. He had been so badly injured 'it was thought his mind had been affected'. On the preceding Friday evening, Agnew locked himself in the toilet of Cassell & Co. on Ludgate Hill, where he was employed as a compositor. When the door was forced open he was found with a bullet wound in his head and a revolver by his side. A note close by read: 'Dear Sir, – Excuse me leaving to-day without first giving the usual fortnight's notice, but I have received a peremptory summons to go to heaven without delay to set the title-page of the Book of Life. Yours ever, H.J.S. Agnew.' Removed to hospital he died without regaining consciousness; the inquest jury returned a verdict of 'suicide while temporarily insane'.

10 FEBRUARY 1888

Michael Ostrog (a.k.a. Bertrand Ashley, Claude Clayton and Dr Grant), a habitual thief and fraud-ster, was released from Surrey Pauper Lunatic Asylum on this day. Ostrog failed to report for his post-release appointments with the police. By October 1888 Ostrog was a wanted man for his failures to report and his image and description were published in the *Police Gazette*. Ostrog is Chief Constable Macnaghten's third and final named suspect on his 1894 memorandum (see 23 February, p. 38). Macnaghten desribed Ostrog as 'a Russian doctor, and a convict, who was subsequently detained in a lunatic asylum as a homicidal maniac. The man's antecedents were of the worst possible type, and his whereabouts at the time of the murders could never be ascertained.'

METROPOLITAN POLICE DISTRICT.
3.—Convict Supervision Office.—Woodcut portrait and description of Supervisee MICHAEL

OSTROG, *alias* BERTRAND ASHLEY, CLAUDE CLAYTON, and DR. GRANT, Office No. 22550, whose apprehension is sought for failing to report—age 55, height 5 ft. 11 in., complexion dark, hair dark brown, eyes grey, scars right thumb and right shin, two large moles right shoulder and one back of neck, corporal punishment marks ; generally dressed in a semi-clerical suit. A Polish Jew. Was sentenced, 5th January, 1874, at Aylesbury, to 10 years' penal servi-tude and 7 years' police supervision for larceny. Libe-rated on license 25th August, 1883. Again sentenced at the Central Criminal Court, 14th September, 1887, to 6 months' hard labour for larceny. On the 10th March, 1888, he was liberated from the Surrey County Lunatic Asylum, and failed to report.
Warrant issued.
Special attention is called to this dangerous man.
Evans/Skinner Crime Archive

Michael Ostrog's notice from
Police Gazette. (Stewart P. Evans)

11 FEBRUARY 1878

The Royal Arsenal railway station tragedy. Eliza Newman (45), a widow, well known in the Woolwich area for her increasingly bemused wanderings, caused by mental decline after the death of her husband, had been taken to Plumstead Workhouse. Two doctors had declared her 'a harmless lunatic' and, following a successful application to the magistrates, final preparations were made for her removal to the county asylum at Banning Heath. Miss Wilkinson, the workhouse matron, had agreed to take Mrs Newman on the train, but as the train rolled in Mrs Newman threw herself on to the track. Miss Wilkinson grabbed hold of her coat but the material simply ripped off in her hand. The station inspector, Frederick Croft, threw himself off the platform towards Mrs Newman and threw her off the rails. Sadly, the brave railway worker did not clear the tracks himself, was caught by the train and killed instantly. He left a widow and children and a subscription was set up for their aid.

12 FEBRUARY 1889

The conclusions were published of an inquest held at Charing Cross Hospital into the death of Mrs Susan Connorton (58), a charwoman employed at the Constitutional Club. PC George Fennell 391E was on duty in the Strand and attended Mrs Connorton. He stated she said she had been walking along Northumberland Street at about 8 p.m. when she 'heard a noise at the back of me and immediately felt something at my back, and then saw a man close by me with a revolver in his hand'. PC Fennell placed her in a cab and took her to hospital. The culprit was one Henry Edward Halliday, a saloon steward, by all accounts a man of good character. He stated he 'discharged the weapon accidentally while adjusting the lever to prevent it from going off'. The inquest jury returned a verdict of 'manslaughter' and Halliday was committed for trial. Further comment was made about the increased incidence of gun crime in the capital, the coroner going so far as to state he considered it 'perfectly disgraceful for a young man to purchase a revolver, together with 20 cartridges, for *2s 6d*'.

13 FEBRUARY 1891

A nasty discovery was made in the early hours of the morning at 'Swallow Gardens', a dingy railway-arched passage between Chamber Street and Royal Mint Street. PC Thompson 240H turned his bull's-eye lantern on the body of a woman lying on her back with blood gushing from a gash to her throat. He blew his whistle for assistance and Police Sergeant Hyde and PC Hinton were soon on the scene.. Dr Phillips, the H Division surgeon, was sent for. Soon word was on the street that Jack the Ripper was 'up to his old tricks again'. The body was identified as Frances Coles (26), 'an unfortunate' known on the street as 'Carrotty Nell'. A violent ship's stoker named James Thomas 'Tom' Sadler was identified as a man who had been seen in the company of Coles for much of the forty-eight hours previous to her murder. Police soon had him in custody and felt they had the Whitechapel murderer. The case collapsed on grounds of faulty identification and Sadler was released.

14 FEBRUARY 1888

William Hyde (36) appeared at Thames Police Court charged with wilfully breaking the plate glass window (value £2) of the Black Horse Tavern on the Bow Road. Witnessed in the act by a policeman, Hyde was seen to hurl a stone at the window. He did not attempt to run away but rather proclaimed, 'Now you can lock me up!' This was an act carried out in desperation. Hyde had applied to the casual wards in the workhouses at Borough, Whitechapel, Mile End and South Grove but had been refused admission at all of them. Starving hungry and desperately tired, he had smashed the window to get arrested so he could spend the night in the shelter of a cell and be guaranteed some food. As he had already served a week in prison, magistrates discharged Hyde with a warning.

15 FEBRUARY 1889

The findings were published of an inquest conducted at Bermondsey into the death of May Beatrice Williams (15), a nursemaid at Dr Button's, 133 Grange Road. May Williams had not been a good girl: she had stolen from her grandmother on several occasions and had been sent to a rescue home from whence she was placed at Dr Button's. Amelia Morez, the cook, said May had threatened suicide several times, and on the night in question had confided she had 'some trouble on her mind'. This was probably the fact she had been given notice by Dr Button, who did not consider her efficient in the nursery. May had free access to the surgery, but the bottles of milk, quinine and strychnine found in her room had *not* come from there. This was apparently not pursued further in court and the jury gave the verdict of 'suicide while temporarily insane'.

16 FEBRUARY 1888

Catherine Ballard (27) appeared at Thames Police Court charged with being drunk and assaulting her child Kate (3). Constable 249H stated that about 11.45 on Wednesday the 15th he was in Leman Street, Whitechapel, when he saw Catherine drunk and carrying her screaming child. Upon him enquiring what was the matter, the child stopped screaming. He walked away but soon heard the same screams again. He returned and questioned Ballard again, learning that she was using the screaming child to gain sympathy in order to assist her in begging for the 5*d* for her lodgings. Every time Ballard put her hand under her child's skirt, she was pricking her with a pin. The child was taken immediately to the workhouse infirmary and her mother was sentenced to one month with hard labour.

17 FEBRUARY 1888 Prisons and Punishments: Clerkenwell House of Detention

This house of detention was opened at Clerkenwell in 1615 as a form of Bridewell, that is to say, a prison where 'mills, turns, cards and suchlike necessary implements' would employ 'rogues and idlers' in some activity (designed to destroy criminal souls) during their incarceration. Burnt down by prisoners in 1679, it was rebuilt shortly afterwards and enlarged in the mid-1770s as an overflow for Newgate Prison. In 1780 it was set alight and its prisoners released by Gordon rioters. Rebuilding and major expansion works were carried out in 1818 and 1846, when its name was changed to the Clerkenwell House of Detention. Even in the mid-nineteenth century the House was described as 'a cramped, dank and horrible hole of misery'. During this period Clerkenwell was the busiest prison in London. Prisoners were mostly only held here for short periods pending trial, and with them were what could be best described as the flotsam of the penal system, that is, army deserters, dishonest cabmen, failed suicides and prisoners awaiting surety (monies to bind prisoners to good behaviour, which could take poor families months to muster). Holding, at capacity, 240 prisoners, in its last ten years an average of 7,000 prisoners passed through Clerkenwell's cells a year. It is estimated that about 200 of them were aged 12 or less. Hundreds of the prisoners were people who were mentally deficient or guilty of petty offences like stealing food because they were hungry; they were far from criminals in the modern sense of the word. In 1867 a Fenian named Michael Barratt blew up a barrel of gunpowder beside the prison in an attempt to release two fellow Fenians imprisoned within. He failed in his mission but he did breach the prison

Clerkenwell House of Detention, *c.* 1875.

wall and destroyed the row of houses opposite, killing six and injuring about fifty others. Barratt was captured, tried, found guilty and hanged at Newgate on 26 May 1868, and he has the grim distinction to have been the last man to be publicly executed in England. Clerkenwell House of Detention was finally closed when local prisons came under the central control of the Prison Commissioners in 1877.

18 FEBRUARY Tales from the Abyss: 'The Blind Beggar Gang'

Known by the name of their regular drinking haunt, the Blind Beggar pub in Bethnal Green, this gang of bullies, 'dips' (pickpockets) and extortionists worked away from their home patch and exploited the more affluent territories of the racetracks and West End. One of their most notorious 'hits' occurred on one election night, when one of their number made his way through cheering crowds to congratulate the victorious Tory candidate on the steps of the Carlton Club. After giving him a generous pat on the back the gang member also relieved the victor of his watch and chain! The gang received a setback in 1891 when, during an anti-Semitic attack on Mr and Mrs Fred Klein, the ferrule of gang member Paul Vaughan's umbrella was accidentally jabbed into Mr Klein's eye. What was meant as a jeering attack resulted in Mr Klein's death. Vaughan was found guilty of manslaughter and he was sent down for seven years.

Mabel Gray, high-society prostitute.

19 FEBRUARY People of the Streets: The Common Prostitute or 'Unfortunate'

It has been estimated that as many as 80,000 prostitutes worked the streets of London in 1888. As many as one in eight women in the East End saw prostitution as their main source of income, a figure that would be higher if one included the women who occasionally turned to 'the oldest trade' when on hard times. In late nineteenth-century London there were distinct types of streetwalkers. The youngest, prettiest girls, who commanded the highest prices, were to be found in the West End. The finest were in Mayfair followed closely by those in Soho and Piccadilly. The 'nice girls' were to be found around Hyde Park, Bayswater, Victoria and Maida Vale, while the 'cheaper girls' were found around Euston and King's Cross. When

Elizabeth Lock, East End 'unfortunate'.

they were too old, too diseased, too drunk or 'too unfortunate' they could well end up as an 'East End Floosie'. Prostitutes in their twenties, like Mary Kelly (the Ripper's final victim), were unusual in the East End. Most were broken older women in their late thirties, forties and fifties (if they lived that long). Prices varied too; pounds could be lavished on the West End girls, whereas half a crown to ten shillings was good going for the street women of the East End. Most of the older women would be happy with the price of a night in a doss house (about threepence) or even a loaf of stale bread for their services.

20 FEBRUARY 1888

Thomas Bennett (44) appeared before Middlesex Sessions to 'be dealt with as an incorrigible rogue and vagabond'. An officer of the mendacity society proved four previous convictions. It was stated in court that Bennett was a well-known beggar and frequently went begging with children that 'he borrowed for the occasion'. He was sentenced to twelve months with hard labour.

21 FEBRUARY Life and Death in the Abyss: Animals

The people of the East End were constantly exposed to animal deaths. In addition to the low average human life expectancy caused by substandard living conditions, poor diet and consequent poor physical health, the death and maltreatment of animals was a daily fact of life as sheep and cattle were driven through the streets to the slaughterhouses clustered in Aldgate, Spitalfields and Whitechapel. Much comment was made in the press and by Christian churchmen on the deterioration of the souls and morals of people exposed to such scenes. John Law recorded the following in *In Darkest London* (1889): 'He . . . saw a herd of frightened sheep being driven over the sawdust into the slaughter house. Their bleating was piteous! At their feet ran a dog barking. Men in blue coats drove them along with sticks, callous of their terror and distress. Many people of the East End enjoy these sights. Some will climb a wall to see a bullock stunned by a pike, or a calf's throat cut.'

22 FEBRUARY Criminal Types: The Garotter

The garotter was a criminal type found predominantly among female felons, who had more chance of getting close to their victims by posing as prostitutes. She would take her target into a suitably dark alley and either punch him hard in the throat or an accomplice would come from behind with a scarf or similar ligature, quickly flip it round the victim's neck and with a rapid jerk render him temporarily insensible while the 'prostitute' robbed him of his wallet, watch and chain. This means of robbery became so common that leather anti-garotte neck stocks were sold and even *Punch* satirised the crime:

> The old 'Stand and deliver's' all rot
> Three to one; hit behind; with a wipe round the jowl, boys,
> That's the ticket, and Vive la Garrotte

An all-female garotter gang in action!

23 February 1894

Sir Melville Macnaghten, Chief Constable CID and second in command to Dr Robert Anderson, writes his confidential and now famous report naming Druitt (see 31 December, p. 191), Ostrog and Kosminski (see 15 July, p. 107 and 6 December, p. 182) as prime Ripper suspects. When considering the likelihood of suspects put forward in this report, it must always be remembered that Macnaghten took up his post with the Metropolitan Police in June 1889 and was not involved with the Ripper investigation of 1888.

24 February People of the Streets: The Policeman

In the late nineteenth century all police officers joining the Metropolitan Police had to be of good health, between the ages of 21 and 27 years and not be less than 5ft 9in in height. Preference for recruitment was always shown towards those from a military background with a good service record. All applicants had to produce letters of recommendation from respectable members of society, such as doctors or clergymen. Medical examinations took place at Scotland Yard and basic training, which consisted of three weeks as a 'candidate on probation' at the candidates' section house in Kennington Lane, included twice-daily squad exercises and foot drill on the parade ground at Wellington Barracks, learning from the instruction book of duties, laws and regulations, followed by a period on beat patrol shadowing experienced constables or sergeants. At the end of their training candidates were sworn in and attested. When going to their beat duties, the fresh patrol would leave the police station and march in file along the kerb to their assigned points while led by their sergeant. The police officers then patrolled their beats at a regulated pace and met up with their colleagues at set points during their hours of duty. Policemen carried a truncheon (slightly longer than the type carried by their descendants in the twentieth century), a Hudson whistle (to raise alarms) with an issue number stamped on it, and a pair of Hiatt's barrel handcuffs. They may even have had a 'snap' or 'come along' twist-and-hold cuff for awkward customers. At night they were issued with a bull's-eye lamp that contained a reservoir of paraffin or oil. It could be either carried or clipped over the belt, and a square of leather protected the policeman's uniform from scorching or stains. The lamp was so designed that the inner shell of the lamp would rotate and block the light to the bull's eye if the vent caps on the top were twisted. Most old sweat coppers appreciated the lamp because they could keep their hands warm on it.

PC 366H. Walter Harris. Joining the force in June 1884 he was one of the H Division constables who trod the streets of Whitechapel throughout the Ripper investigation. His beat covered some of the toughest neighbourhoods in London and it finally dragged him down too – Harris was dismissed in 1895 for being drunk and in disarray.

25 FEBRUARY 1888

Annie Millwood (38) was attacked and stabbed about the legs and lower torso by a strange man with a clasp knife. She survived her ordeal but said she did not recognise her attacker. No witnesses came forward and her attacker was never caught. She recovered from her wounds and was discharged from South Grove Workhouse on 21 March. She was at this workhouse again on 31 March when she collapsed and died following a rupture of her left pulmonary artery that was caused by advanced ulceration.

26 FEBRUARY 1896

The last triple execution at Newgate of murderers Seaman, Milsom and Fowler. Seaman was convicted of the 'Turner Street Murders' in Whitechapel. While attempting a robbery at the home of John Goodman Levy (77), Seaman was disturbed by the old man, who he stabbed and battered. The housekeeper, Mrs Gale, was found murdered in the bedroom. The intruder had been observed entering and the police were summoned. A large crowd assembled outside but no one saw the intruder leave. Detective Sergeant Wensley saw a hole in the bedroom ceiling and spotted another in the roof – Seaman was on the tiles! Realising the game was up, Seaman threw himself off the roof at the crowd below. It was a 40ft drop and he broke both thighs. He was joined on the gallows by Harry Fowler and Albert Milsom, who had killed the elderly Henry Smith while attempting to burgle his Muswell Hill home. James Billington was assisted in the execution by William Warbrick. Both burglars had intended to turn King's evidence on each other and intense animosity was apparent between them to the extent that Fowler violently attacked Milsom in the court while the jury were making their deliberations. At the execution Seaman was put between the two, and as he took his place in the drop he exclaimed, 'First time I've ever been a bloody peacemaker.' Working so rapidly, and no doubt relieved to have the three men on the drop without incident, Billington released the trap but did not see that his assistant Warbrick had not cleared and he plunged into the pit. Warbrick held on to the legs of the man he was nearest to and swung into the pit, thus avoiding a nasty accident.

27 FEBRUARY 1872

Most of us know the pain and discomfort of a bad bout of diarrhoea. People in unsanitary Victorian Britain were all too familiar with the symptoms of extreme diarrhoea combined with escalating fever caused by 'filth disease' or typhoid. When Queen Victoria's beloved son Bertie, the Prince of Wales (later King Edward VII), contracted typhoid, the disease which had claimed her dear husband Albert almost exactly eleven years before, it was a matter of national concern. He had such a bad dose of the disease it was a small miracle that he recovered. The Queen declared a day of national thanksgiving for his recovery. Special supplements were dedicated to the subject in newspapers and magazines, the streets of London were decked with bunting and the streets of the capital were lined with cheering crowds along the route taken by the royal carriages and escorts to and from St Paul's Cathedral.

Queen Victoria's beloved son Bertie, the Prince of Wales (later Edward VII), *c.* 1872.

28 February People of the Streets: The Olive and Gherkin Seller

On the main and side streets of Whitechapel and Spitalfields could be found shops selling olives and gherkins. These wares were displayed on a ledge which was lowered like a drawbridge when the shop opened, in big wooden tubs and were mostly bought and eaten on the spot. Along these little streets could also be found shops selling light refreshments for Russians and Romanian Jews. The tiny shop openings were ornamented with Yiddish menus written in Hebrew characters.

29 FEBRUARY 1888

Ann Mary Randle (29) was indicted at the Central Criminal Court for administering poison to her son Samuel Everleigh Randle with intent to murder him. Randle was a widow who lived with her four children on Lower Road, Richmond; their rent was in arrears to the tune of £30 and they faced eviction. Desperate, she gave all the children laudanum; police were summoned when she began screaming out 'take me away' and threatening she would bite the veins in her arm and bleed to death. However, the laudanum only made the children sick, and therefore the court decided that it had been administered to create sympathy. Randle was discharged.

Cells and stairs inside Newgate Prison.

MARCH

A police ambulance litter, *c.* 1888. One of the most unpopular duties for policemen was ambulance duty because it could entail anything from picking up a vomiting and incapable drunk and taking them to the station, to the recovery of accident and murder victims. On such a device most of the victims of Jack the Ripper were removed from the scenes of crime. If the ambulance was fully covered it was common knowledge a dead body was inside and it would draw attention and comment as it was wheeled through the streets. Children would find amusement in following the drops of blood which would frequently drip from the litter leaving a trail all the way to the mortuary.

1 MARCH 1892

James Muir (39), a shoemaker from Whitechapel, was executed at Newgate by James Billington. Muir had recently left his paramour, Abigail Sullivan, after a drunken row. Muir soon took up with another woman at another residence but Sullivan would not leave him alone and even pestered him for money at his place of work. Muir gave her short shrift, but he brooded on her behaviour and went to see her after work at her residence on Old Nicol Street, Bethnal Green. He was told to leave but he refused, and, enraged by his treatment, he stabbed her in the breast with a butcher's knife. His arrest was swift and his punishment almost a foregone conclusion.

2 MARCH People of the Streets: Costers

Costermongers, colloquially known simply as 'costers', were mostly smallholders who had wheeled stalls or 'barra's' on many of the main roads and side turnings around the capital; for the traders of Whitechapel this was the Goulston Street (where the 'Juwes' graffiti was discovered) and Wentworth Street area. Every sort of commodity, be it clothes, food, plates, bowls or cheap ornaments, could be obtained from the costers – and rather like their shopkeeping counterparts they opened early and traded into the hours of darkness. Their only real day off was a Sunday when they would don their best for walking out, many of them adopting the distinctive garb of 'Pearly King and Queen', with their coats and hats covered in small pearl shirt and dress buttons. The women wore huge hats with ostrich plumes, purple plush dresses, spotless white aprons and yellow boots.

The bustling Goulston Street/Petticoat Lane market, *c.* 1890.

3 MARCH 1880

If he could have said, 'I told you so'! An inquest was held at the Prince of Wales Tavern, Bonner Road, Bethnal Green, on the body of Edgar Tiddeman (60). Tiddeman had long suffered with diseases of the heart and liver and had been advised by friends to go to the workhouse infirmary, but he had always declared if he were to do so it would be his death. Friends persisted and obtained him a place in the infirmary, and they had an ambulance sent for him. He would not get in it at his own door, but said that if they went a little way on he would follow them. This was done, but when the old man reached the ambulance he fell back into the arms of the assistants and immediately expired. The verdict of inquest was that 'excitement of removal to workhouse had accelerated death'.

4 MARCH 1880

Reports appeared of the inquest held at the White Lion, High Street, Shadwell, where the body of John William Todminster (13) was viewed by an inquest jury. The lad, who lived with his parents at 99 George Street East, had attempted to get on the shaft of the dustcart on New Gravel Lane. In doing so he touched the reins and caused the horses to start. The boy was immediately thrown to the ground and the wheels passed over his head, killing him on the spot. The jury returned a verdict of accidental death.

5 MARCH 1891

Thomas Henry Cutbush was taken into Lambeth Infirmary and detained as a lunatic. He escaped within hours and over the following four days until he was captured again he stabbed Florrie Johnson in the buttocks and attempted to repeat the deed on Isabelle Anderson. Charged with malicious wounding, Cutbush spent the rest of his life in Broadmoor Criminal Lunatic Asylum, where he died in 1903. In February 1894 the *Sun* newspaper made the suggestion that Cutbush and Jack the Ripper were one and the same. This matter was thoroughly investigated and Cutbush was not considered a likely suspect at all. This investigation did however lead directly to the Macnaghten memorandum (see 23 February, p. 38), which dismisses Cutbush and names the now infamous three suspects: Druitt, Kosminski and Ostrog.

6 MARCH 1900

The execution was carried out at Newgate of Ada Chard Williams (24) for the murder of Selina Ellen Jones, a child which had been placed in her care. Williams was another baby farmer and was exposed after the body of a baby wrapped up in a parcel was washed up on the banks of the Thames in Battersea and identified by her mother as 21-month-old Selina Jones. This baby had been placed in the hands of Chard Williams, who, for a fee, had agreed to find the babe a new home. Chard Williams saw the report in the press. She did not wait to be traced, but she wrote a letter to the

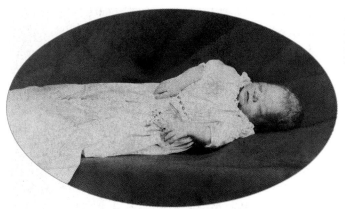

An example of the Victorian vogue for photographing the dead. Child mortality was high but baby farmers were still kept busy.

police admitting she was baby farming but denying any knowledge of the child's murder. She and her husband were both arrested. He was considered more an accomplice than a murderer and charges were not pursued against him, but Chard Williams was found guilty and sentenced to death. Although she was only charged with this one horrible death, other bundles of unrelated baby clothes were discovered when police searched her house, all tied with the same knot as the parcel poor little Selina had been wrapped in. . . .

7 MARCH 1889

An inquest was held at the City Coroner's Court, Golden Lane, regarding the death of David Danby (37), landlord of the Rose and Crown, Little Britain, Aldergate Street. The story emerged of how Danby had argued with Alfred Cornwall (33), his brother-in-law, over 10s missing from the takings. The dispute escalated to the extent Danby came at Cornwall with a poker. Cornwall carried a loaded revolver. Fearing great harm from the considerably bigger Danby, Cornwall discharged four shots at Danby before he was brought down. Cornwall immediately ran into the street and called for the police. Tried at the Old Bailey, Cornwall was found guilty of manslaughter and sent down for ten years' penal servitude.

8 MARCH 1888

Mrs Eliza Ann Smith (26) appeared at Thames Police Court for attempting to procure a girl, Kate Spencer (under 21 years), to become a prostitute. Also charged in the case was Eliza Millings (alias Pea) the keeper of a brothel at 3 Ernest Street, Stepney. Smith had induced the Spencer girl to come to London 'to seek a husband' and paid her fare from Gloucester. Smith met Spencer in London and took her to the house on Ernest Street. Over tea, when Spencer explained she had no money for rent to stay there and had nowhere else to stay Millings, had said, 'You had better go out and get men and money.' In the evening the girl was taken by Millings to the Paragon Music Hall to meet and attract clients. Spencer started crying. Luckily PC Barnes 280H was on duty and enquired of the young girl what was wrong and the whole sordid story spilled out.

Millings and Smith were soon apprehended, found guilty of their crimes and sentenced, respectively, to two years and one-and-a-half years with hard labour.

9 MARCH Prisons and Punishments: Coldbath Fields

Coldbath Fields was built in 1794 with the intention of making it a prison to hold and set vagrants to work. Its original purpose was soon obscured through necessity and Coldbath Fields became a gaol for petty offenders. Made infamous for its brutal regime, labour for prisoners here was specifically designed as a punishment rather than an educative or corrective activity. Here were six treadwheel yards with a total of twenty wheels. Each prisoner was set a target of 1,200 feet on the wheel each day and woe betide those who did not achieve it! Coldbath Fields expanded over the years to become the largest prison in England with a total capacity of 1,700 prisoners; at least half of those incarcerated here were petty offenders or those who had failed to pay small fines. Following the centralisation of the Prison Commissioners in 1877, Coldbath Fields Prison was on borrowed time and it finally closed in 1885. It was demolished in 1889 and Mount Pleasant post office now occupies the site.

'You had better go out and get men and money.'

10 MARCH 1888

James Bailey (45) and Alfred Bailey (5) appeared at Thames Police Court on charges of begging. The magistrate, Mr Saunders, 'The Hammer of Vagrants and Foreigners', sentenced the father to seven days' imprisonment and ordered the boy to be sent to the workhouse. His justification for dividing father and son: 'It is perfectly absurd to charge a child of 5 years with begging, because he happened to be in the arms of his father.'

The main gate to Coldbath Fields Prison, c. 1875.

11 MARCH 1887

Mrs Samuels was found bludgeoned in her shop on Bartholomew Road, Kentish Town. Just before 4 p.m. several men were seen to drive up in a cart. Those who noticed the trap thought the men were visiting the nearby pub and paid no further notice. A short while later the trap was noticed to have driven off and poor Mrs Samuels was found lying in the street doorway with her head smashed with the likes of a crowbar. They had attempted to remove her 2cwt iron safe, but this had been dropped nearby. Nobody was ever apprehended for this dreadful crime.

12 MARCH People of the Streets: Hot Pie Sellers

The selection of hot pies available in the East End was unrivalled in any other part of London. To be had here were pies of hot beef-steak, eels, kidney, meat, fruit and mincemeat. Dressed in his distinctive clean white apron, the pieman would lift the lid on the metal receptacle in front of him on his cart with nimble deftness, whip out a hot pie, run a knife around the inside of the dish and turn it out on to a piece of paper for his customer. On busy nights he was joined by his wife and daughter, each with their own pie warmers. 'If you watch long enough it will almost appear to you that a shower of hot pies is being flung up from below by an invisible agency.'

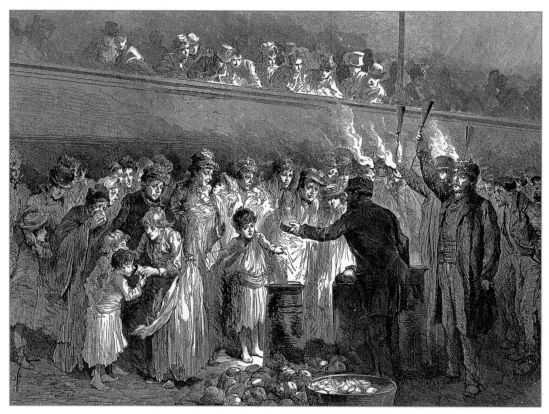

Hot pies for all!

13 MARCH 1889

The conclusion of an adjourned inquest held at St Nicholas School, Deptford, into the death of Alice Evans (43), wife of a lighterman, living at 37 Deptford Green. She was confined on 17 February and attended by Mrs Wykes the midwife. When she complained of extreme pain, William Bowden (31), an unqualified assistant to Dr Macnaughton was called. Bowden prescribed for her but 'thought there was no immediate danger'. She died later the same day of a condition diagnosed post-mortem as puerperal fever. The inquest concluded with accusations of gross ignorance against Bowden for 'acting as a medical man without licence'. At the ensuing trial there was 'not sufficient evidence to prove criminal negligence' and Bowden was acquitted.

14 MARCH Life and Death in the Abyss: The Workhouse

One of the last resorts for the desperate homeless of Whitechapel was a stay in the casual ward of the Whitechapel Workhouse, colloquially known as 'The Spike'. Places were limited and queueing to enter for the night began from about 1 p.m., though no one was admitted until 6 p.m. People were admitted in groups of three. Each person would be asked their name, age, occupation, place of birth and condition of destitution and were searched for money, knives, matches or tobacco. If they were found to have money, they would be sent out to buy their doss elsewhere, and all other items would be confiscated. Once inside, a 'brick' of bread would be pressed in their hands, which they would eat after dipping it in the heaps of salt scattered over the filthy wooden tables where they sat on benches to eat. A pannikin containing three-quarters of a pint

The Whitechapel Workhouse, known on the streets as 'The Spike', *c.* 1895.

of 'skilly' (a mixture of Indian corn and hot water) was also provided, and the taste of this mix was recorded as 'unseasoned, gross and bitter'. To get this heavy stodge of food down, water could be drawn by the pint. Before retiring all would bathe; two baths were provided and over twenty vagrants with all manner of illness, infestations and sores would bathe in the *same* water. Issued with a nightshirt (worn by untold others as evidenced by the smell and stains), the inmates would retire to sleep on canvas strips 6ft long and less than 2ft wide, set about 6in apart and 8in above the floor. The stench of so many crammed in together was 'frightful and sickening'. If people got any sleep they could well be disturbed by a rat scuttling over them. When the morning came they would rise at six, have a similar breakfast to dinner and earn their place from the previous night by a labour-intensive job, such as stone-breaking, picking oakum, cleaning or food preparation, set by the workhouse taskmasters. Many thought this life was no better than serving a gaol sentence.

15 MARCH 1888

An inquest was resumed at the Railway Tavern, Deptford, into the death of the two infants found in a basket in a third-class railway carriage at New Cross Station. Over three adjourned hearings the tragic tale unfolded of Edith Tilley (19), a waitress who became somewhat unbalanced after the birth of her two illegitimate children, Daisy and Edith. The inquest concluded on 19 March deciding the babes had been accidentally suffocated and abandoned in terror by their unstable mother.

16 MARCH People of the Streets: Musicians

The busy streets of London were frequently filled with musical entertainers hoping to raise a few 'bob'. There were various kinds. The solo performers or duos would regale passers-by with tunes on a vast array of instruments, such as tin whistles, concertinas, harps, violins, but the king of the soloists was the bagpiper, who was usually turned out in plaid. The skill of playing this instrument was respected by all other performers. Many players were tall, ex-military types and really cut quite a dash on the streets. There were even violin quartettes and small bands, which were invariably from the German immigrant population. The man who seems to linger most in the popular psyche is the one-man band, with his brass hat with bells, panpipes, accordion, big drum and cymbals. The skill of mastering this complicated rigout was handed down from generation to generation and its secrets never divulged to others. In Victorian times the standard of the performers was quite high, due to the disapproving public being pretty unforgiving if it wasn't. Money would not be forthcoming, but abuse, rubbish, dung and fists would soon fly aplenty to quieten offensive rackets.

17 MARCH Life and Death in the Abyss: 'Carrying the Banner'

If there was no room in the casual ward of the workhouse, the homeless of East London would have to 'carry the banner', that is, stay awake all night, walking the

'Little more than rag sacks
of humanity.'

streets for a discreet hiding place to sleep in. The law was clear, no person was allowed
to be found asleep on the street; if they were discovered by a passing policeman, they
would be shaken awake and sent on their way. It was widely known among those who
'carried the banner' that Green Park was one of the earliest to open its gates, so rain or
shine the homeless would pour in and soon every available bench would become a day
bed for one who had been up all night. If no bench was found, the tired vagrants
would simply lay on the wet, dewy grass. During the daytime the Spitalfields Garden,
which was situated in the shadow of Christ's Church, was another haunt of the homeless and dispossessed of the East End. Here could be found whole families who were
'little more than rag sacks of humanity' huddled together and asleep on the benches.
Many of the vagrants here were filthy dirty and heavily infested with lice and sores; it
was little wonder that the Spitalfield's Garden was known locally as 'Itchy Park'.

18 MARCH 1889

Louis Diemshutz (27) (see 30 September, p. 144), unlicensed hawker of 40 Berner
Street, Samuel Friedman, cap blocker of 81 Weaver Street, Spitalfields, and Isaac
Kozebrodski (19), a machinist of 40 Old Ford Road, Bethnal Green, appeared at
Thames Police Court charged with being 'disorderly persons and concerned together' in
assaulting Israel Sunshine, Isaac Solomons, Emanuel Snapper and Emanuel Jacobs.
They were further charged with assaulting PCs James Frost 154H and George Harris
269H while in execution of their duty. The incident occurred after the dispersal of a
procession of the Jewish unemployed in the East End. The crowd had set off from

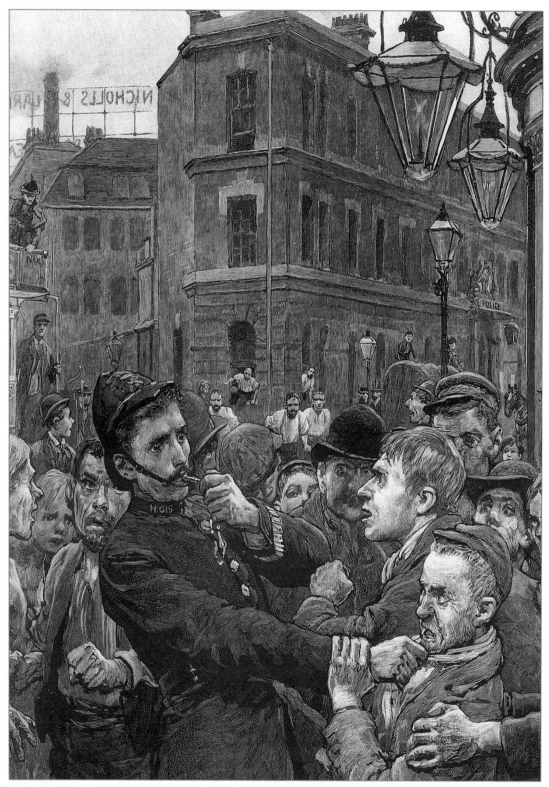

A 'thump up' in the East End, *c.* 1889. The building in the background is the Commercial Street Police Station. *(Stewart P. Evans)*

outside the International Working Men's Club (where Diemshutz was Steward), but after the march many who were not members had returned to the club and attempted unsuccessfully to gain entry. Taking offence at this, a crowd of between 100 and 200 gathered outside and started throwing stones, hooting and banging on the door. Diemshutz sent for the police, but as they arrived the club members assumed the defensive and charged the crowd, hitting them with broomsticks, walking sticks and umbrellas. PC Frost was in plain clothes and attempted to arrest Diemshutz, who was clearly one of the leaders of the assault. He was struck and kicked by Diemshutz and others and was dragged into the passage of the club and further assaulted. The trial was sent up to the County of London Sessions. The jury found the accused guilty of the assault on the policemen but acquitted him of other charges. Diemshutz was sentenced to three months' imprisonment with hard labour and bound over after release for twelve months. Kozebrodski was fined £4.

19 MARCH 1888

Hannah Smith, 'a respectfully dressed woman', was indicted at the Old Bailey for abandoning her six-month-old baby. The child had been found on the doorstop of a Mrs Derby, the wife of a Mortlake builder. Alerted to its presence by its cries, she found the baby was warmly wrapped up with a note pushed up its sleeve: 'To Mr Derby Senior. You have driven me to do in my desperation that which will cause me regret as long as I shall live – that is to leave your child at your door. . . . We have both committed a great sin, and you like a coward left me to bear all blame and consequences . . .' It transpired that Miss Smith had called before, had seen Mrs Derby, but the discussion became so heated she was ordered out by Derby's son. Mr Derby flatly denied being the father of the child. The recorder pointed out there was no evidence for reckless abandonment and the jury returned the verdict of not guilty. No decision was made over the paternity of the child. Miss Smith was discharged and a subscription on her behalf was made by the jury, members of the bar and court.

20 MARCH Life and Death in the Abyss: Life in the Tenements

Tenement housing was cramped, dirty, unsanitary and inhumane. For a weekly rent of about four shillings, families of five, six and seven people crammed themselves into these filthy rooms, which were furnished only by a rough, worn table, broken-down bedstead, or more likely a contrivance of boards resting on old wooden crates or bricks, with an unwashed,

Frying Pan Alley, Whitechapel, c. 1895.

flea-infested straw mattress on top and rags for a blanket. Andrew Mearns in *The Bitter Cry of Outcast London* stated these examples among many: 'In one cellar a sanitary inspector reports finding a father, mother, three children and four pigs! In another room a missionary found a man ill with small-pox, his wife just recovering from her eighth confinement, and the children running around half naked and covered with dirt. Here are seven people living in one underground kitchen, and a little dead child in the same room. Elsewhere is a poor widow, her three children, and a child who had been dead thirteen days. Her husband, who was a cabman, had shortly before committed suicide.'

21 MARCH 1887

Joseph King was executed at Newgate. King, a bricklayer by trade, shared a lodging house with a number of individuals and families at 19 Hart Street, Grosvenor Square. Among the other residents were a pretty young lady named Annie Sutton and her illegitimate son, Harry. King had asked Annie out a few times but she had politely refused. They remained on friendly terms but King persisted and began to delude himself she would, eventually, say yes to him. On 20 January King learnt that Annie had accepted a date with another lodger and a furious row erupted between them. On hearing hideous cries of 'Murder!' from the room, Charles Stanfield, another lodger, entered just in time to observe King sawing at the child's throat with a razor, while Annie lay dying nearby with her throat cut. After a desperate struggle in which Stanfield received some bad cuts, he managed to wrestle King into his room, locked the door and summoned the police. At his trial, King attempted to blame an old head wound and a type of sunstroke for his actions, but this weak defence cut no ice with the jury, and he was sentenced to death.

22 MARCH 1880

John Wingfield (34), a labourer, was executed at Newgate for the murder of his wife in full view of a crowd of people, at which the press was outraged. *The Times* was moved to state, 'The crime was committed in circumstances of remarkable atrocity, for the prisoner, who was very jealous of his wife, met her in broad daylight in the streets of Kilburn and there in the presence of a crowd of people, who were too horrified or too cowardly to interpose, inflicted no fewer than 17 wounds upon her, from which she died.' The defence pleaded insanity, but Wingfield was convicted. He behaved in an exemplary manner as a prisoner, his despatch at the hands of executioner Marwood passed without incident.

23 MARCH 1888

Eliza Pearman (32) of 43 Ettrick Street, Poplar, was charged at Thames Police Court with keeping a disorderly house. It was revealed she had been summoned before for a similar offence. She was sentenced to two months with hard labour.

Interior of the Thames Police Court, *c.* 1895.

24 MARCH 1879

The mannered murderer. James Simms (43), a former American seaman, was executed at Newgate for the murder of Lucy Graham, 'a woman of loose character', in a public house at Shadwell. Simms had been 'paid off' from his ship in the port of London. With his money burning a hole in his pocket and plenty of people to help him spend it, the money was soon gone (or possibly stolen). When Simms saw Lucy Graham (a woman he claimed had stolen his money at a previous assignation), he struck out and cut her throat with a razor in a fit of desperate and bitter revenge. Resigned to his fate, Simms was a model prisoner who went to the scaffold with a firm step. As the cap was pulled over his head, he said he wished to speak to the prison governor. He said, 'I wish to thank you, Sir, in particular, and also all the rest of the officers, for your great kindness. I am satisfied; that is all.' The bolt was drawn, the trap fell and Simms died instantly.

25 MARCH 1877

William Saunders (34) was found dead, having been kicked to death and thrown into a pond near Penge Cricket Club. Saunders had been seen arguing with his lodger, James Dempsey, the evening before his body was discovered. Saunders's wife and other family members made 'unsatisfactory' statements, or changed them, about what they saw and what their movements were on the night in question. It soon became evident that probably two men closely associated with the family had been involved, but due to the confusion of statements and the time wasted in the investigation (there were no forensic procedures in 1877), there was no chance of a conviction.

26 MARCH 1890

John Neal (64) was executed at Newgate. Neal, a bricklayer, had married a considerably younger woman named Theresa and had recently moved to new lodgings at 81 St Peter Street, Islington. Four days after their arrival a jealous row erupted. Drawing his pocket-knife, Neal swung at Theresa and caused a deep puncture wound to her neck, from which she died in seconds. He was found guilty of murder and sentenced to death. As executioner Berry made his final preparations, Neal said his last words: 'I'm sorry I committed the murder but she was a bad wife to me.'

27 MARCH 1888

Louis Heilfink (37), who described himself as 'a teacher of music' at 57 Tachbrook Street, Pimlico, appeared at Westminister Court charged with abducting and assaulting Caroline Seilberge. Seilberge stated that on 14 March she had left her home in Rotterdam with Heilfink, who had said he was a merchant with a house in London, on a promise that he would marry her. On arrival she was taken to a brothel and compelled to work the streets and pay Heilfink, to whom she was now 'in his debt for the fare and lodgings'. When she returned home without money or not enough she was beaten. On the 25th she returned without any money and Heilfink beat and kicked her and literally threw her out on to the street. Lost and bewildered, Seilberge wandered the streets until she encountered a police officer. Heilfink was bailed on two sureties of £25 each.

28 MARCH 1888

At approximately 2.30 a.m. Ada Wilson, a seamstress, was about to retire to bed at her lodgings at 9 Maidman Street, Burdett Road, Mile End, when there was a knock on the street door. There stood a man of about 30 years of age, 5ft 6in tall, wearing a wideawake hat. He demanded money from Ada and stated that if she did not comply immediately, she had just moments to live. Ada flatly refused and received two stab wounds in the throat from a clasp knife. Her gurgling screams brought the neighbourhood running and put her assailant to flight. Police and a Dr Wheeler were soon on the scene. She was removed to the London Hospital where she was fortunate enough to recover from her wounds. Despite giving a description, and a witness coming forward to confirm her story, Ada Wilson's attacker was never traced.

29 MARCH 1892

John Noble (46), a chimney sweep, was executed at Newgate for the murder of Mary Elizabeth Swift, the woman he had been living with for the last four years. When she told Noble she was leaving him, he cut her throat with a razor, but she was just able to run across the road to the pub, where she collapsed and died. Noble walked determinedly and unaided to the gallows, and his last words echoed those of the Revd

G.P. Merrick, the prison chaplain: 'Lord Jesus have mercy on my soul.' The executioner was the newly appointed James Billington; the length of drop was recorded at 7ft 4in; death was instantaneous.

30 MARCH Prisons and Punishments: Wormwood Scrubs

This prison was built by convict labour and completed in 1890. The bricks were made from clay on the site and the stone came from Dartmoor and Portland prison quarries. Portland also provided iron castings, while carpenters, joiners and blacksmiths were found among the prisoners of Millbank and Chatham. Over 7,030 prisoners assisted in the construction. They stayed in wooden barrack huts with the perimeter of the site guarded by ex-soldier civilians armed with rifles; only one prisoner escaped during the construction work. Intended for 1,000 inmates, it was, at the time, the largest prison in Britain. Both men and women serving short sentences were held in separate wings of the prison. Unlike other prisons of the time, the inside was commodious and well ventilated to guard against gaol fever or typhoid. Prisoners here worked the old staples of picking oakum, treadmills and cranks, but they also learnt new skills, making shoes, sacks and post office bags. Wormwood Scrubs still exists as a prison today.

Women prisoners, carrying their babies, walk the prescribed trackways of the exercise yard of Wormwood Scrubs, *c.* 1895

31 MARCH 1898

The death of Eleanor Marx-Aveling, favourite daughter of Karl Marx, the father of communism. Eleanor Marx followed proudly in her father's footsteps and championed the socialist cause with a passion and was widely known for her work across the East End (she even spoke in the meeting hall opposite 29 Hanbury Street). After Karl's death in 1883, Eleanor became involved with Dr Edward Aveling, a man described by Friedrich Engels' biographer as a man with 'the thieving instincts of a jackdaw and the morals of a tom-cat', but Eleanor would not be turned from him. Although not married to him, she was 'devoted to the point of slavery' and adopted his surname with her own. Her death is surrounded with some mystery. On the morning of 31 March a note was taken by a woman claiming to be Aveling's maid to a Sydenham chemist stating, 'Please give the bearer chloroform and a small quantity of prussic acid for the dog.' Dr Aveling's card was enclosed. Curiously, the chemist's poison book was initialled E.M.A. Later that same morning, dressed all in white, Eleanor was found dead on her bed. At the inquest Aveling's answers were 'evasive', but the verdict of suicide was delivered. A twist to the tale came a few years later, when it was rumoured that Aveling had deceived Eleanor into a suicide pact, but he did not keep his side of the bargain. We will probably never know the truth.

APRIL

London Bridge, *c.* 1895. Scene of history for centuries, heads of executed felons and treasonous gentry were once displayed on spikes here and many a suicide has gazed their last here as they plunged over the parapet into the arms of 'Old Father' Thames.

1 APRIL, 1898

This was a strangely appropriate day to die for Arthur Orton, the 'Tichbourne Claimant', one of the nineteenth century's most notorious fraudsters. Orton had come to public notice after Lady Tichbourne advertised for news of her long-lost son, Sir Roger. Orton, a Wapping butcher's son living in Wagga-Wagga, Australia, answered, claiming to be the lost son himself! Despite Orton being 27 stone, when Sir Roger was last seen weighing 9 stone, and all evidence of his Stonyhurst accent gone, Lady T. was delighted to have her son back. Relatives and friends of Sir Roger had less clouded views and took Orton to court. What ensued was the longest case in British judicial history – a total of 1,025 days. Orton's case finally collapsed with the testimony of Lord Bellow, an old schoolfriend of Sir Roger. Bellow knew Sir Roger had a tattoo on his left forearm – Orton had nothing there. After serving a sentence of fourteen years' hard labour, Orton toured the country as a circus sideshow telling his story. He died in poverty, earning a few coppers by displaying himself in Kilburn pubs. Thousands came to see his funeral procession; Orton was buried in a pauper's grave.

2 APRIL, 1888

At Worship Street Court, Francis Sullivan (22), a labourer of Queen Ann Street, Whitechapel, was charged with burglariously entering the Crown and Anchor public house on Cheshire Street, Bethnal Green. He helped himself to eighty-eight half-ounce packets of tobacco, 230 cigars, £1 8s in money and other articles valued at £7 6s, property of the landlord, Mr John Nelson. At about 5.30 on the same morning, PC Kemp 439J saw Sullivan carrying a bag and coat on Cheshire Street, which he deposited inside the door of one of the houses. This suspicious

Whitechapel High Street, *c.* 1888. *(Living London)*

behaviour caused PC Kemp to apprehend the man and enquire his business. Soon the break-in at the pub was discovered and the contents of Sullivan's bag matched the missing goods. Offering no defence, Sullivan was sent to the Central Criminal Court for trial.

3 April, 1888

Emma Elizabeth Smith (45) was robbed and assaulted on Osborn Street, just off the Whitechapel Road, by three men. She suffered bruising and a cut to her right ear, but her worst injuries were internal. A blunt instrument had been thrust into her vagina with such force it tore her peritoneum. She could not or would not describe or identify her assailants. She died the next day of peritonitis at the London Hospital. Her assailants were never caught. (see also 31 August, p. 128.)

4 April, Prisons and Punishments: 'Broad Arrow Men'

A familiar term for prisoners in the late nineteenth and early twentieth century was 'broad arrow men', an epithet gained from the distinctive broad arrow or 'crow's foot' stamped on to all prison uniforms. The origins of the symbol go back to the seventeenth century when a master of the ordnances in the Tower of London began

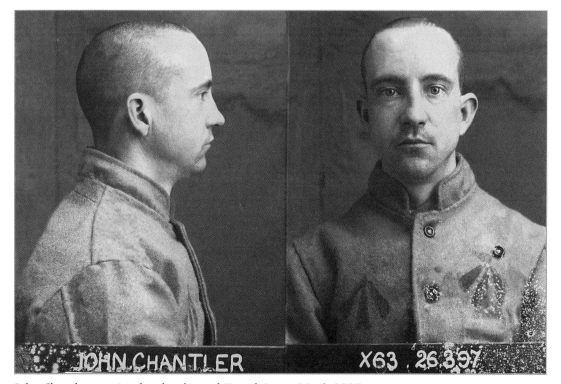

John Chantler, convicted embezzler and 'Broad Arrow Man', 1897.

marking the weaponry as Tower property with an arrow-like device from his coat of arms. Over the years this symbol has been adopted by all government departments to denote equipment as diverse as military vehicle parts and rifles to rulers and paperweights as government issue. The broad arrow was stamped onto prison garb not only to create a 'dress of shame' to be worn by convicts but to make the clothes they wore so distinctive they would stand out as convicts if they effected an escape. Broad arrows were discontinued on prison uniforms in 1922.

5 April, 1888

Richard Frederick Geere (44), noted as 'well dressed', was charged at Worship Street Court with the embezzlement of three separate sums of £6, £4 17s and £2 10s and other sums received by him on account of his employers Messrs Cavender & Co., tobacconists of 65 Great Eastern Street, Shoreditch. A travelling salesman, Geere was supplied with a pony and trap, paid £2 10s a week and allowed £1 a week expenses. Geere was found not to have accounted for several sums received from customers and was confronted with this. He was suspended and asked to forward a statement of defalcations, in which he set out a total of nearly £180. Upon this admission he was arrested at his home. He claimed extenuating circumstances; a large family to support and an elderly mother dependent on him. The magistrate was lenient and sentenced him to two months' imprisonment with hard labour.

6 April, 1891

During this month George Gissing had his first novel published. Entitled *New Grub Street*, it explored his feelings and experiences of abject poverty. Gissing lived a chaotic and varied life, spending fourteen years of it at a variety of addresses in London. He won scholarships to universities in Manchester and London but frittered his money away living with Nell Harrison, a prostitute, from whom he contracted a venereal disease. He stole from the pockets of his fellow students to support Nell, was caught, expelled from college and sent to prison for a month. His father sent the errant boy to America where he wrote *New Grub Street*, after which he returned to England to marry Nell. They had few years together, for she died in 1888. Driven by pain, desperation and single-mindedness Gissing pushed on to get *New Grub Street* (1891) published. Once this book was out he continued to write *Born in Exile* (1892), *The Odd Women* (1893) and his satirical autobiography *The Private Papers of Henry Pycroft* (1903); he died the same year this was published.

7 April, People of the Streets: The Barrel Organ Men

One of the most evocative sounds of the Victorian street is that of the barrel organ. The organs were Italian-made and gaudily painted, much in the style of the ice-cream stalls, both of which came under the control of the padrones, the Italian owners who hired out the organs for a daily fee. Initially the owners tried to keep the organ grinders all Italian and flatly refused all other applicants. Their stance soon changed when their machines began to be mysteriously damaged. Soon the barrel organ men were also acquiring added attractions for their shows, including dancing monkeys and peg doll puppets (which they would demonstrate and sell). The barrel organ was particularly favoured by amputee ex-soldiers, who, unable to work in farm or factory, would 'wind the barra' wearing faded uniforms and well-rubbed medals rather than beg.

8 April, 1871

Murder in Mayfair. Mme Reil, mistress of Crimean War hero Lord Lucan, was found dead in the cellar pantry at her house at 13 Park Lane. She had been battered to death at the foot of the cellar stair and a rope had been put about her neck so she could be dragged like a side of meat into the more secluded cellar pantry. News of the dreadful deed soon spread – Murder in Mayfair was so uncommon that the last incident of this kind had been thirty years before. It soon became apparent that the Belgian cook, Marguerite Diblanc (29), and some money were missing. Diblanc was traced and extradited from Paris. At her trial it became apparent that Mme Reil was a hard employer and had accused Diblanc of listening at doors and drinking, and summarily dismissed her. The jury agreed there had been extreme provocation and her death sentence was soon commuted to life imprisonment.

9 April, 1882

The death of Dante Gabriel Rossetti, poet, painter and one of the founder members of the Pre-Raphaelite Brotherhood. He has rested in peace ever since, but his wife Elizabeth was not so lucky. She died from a overdose of laudanum in 1862. Overcome with grief for his darling wife, Rossetti buried her with the manuscript and sole copy of the poems he had written to her over the years, nestling it between her cheek and hair. In 1869 Rosetti regretted his emotional gesture and had her exhumed and the book removed from the coffin, along with a long lock of her famous red-gold hair. After disinfection and cleaning, the manuscript, entitled *Poems*, was published in 1870.

10 APRIL, Life and Death in the Abyss: 'Self-neglect'

A case of 'self-neglect' was recorded by Jack London in *People of the Abyss*. Dr Wynn Westcott held an inquest at Shoreditch, respecting the death of Elizabeth Crews, aged 77 years, of 32 East Street, Holborn. She had laid dead and undiscovered for several days. Mr Francis Birch, the relieving officer stated that 'he found the woman in a terrible state, and the ambulance and coachman had to be disinfected after the removal. Dr Chase Fennell said death was due to blood-poisoning from bedsores, due to self-neglect and filthy surroundings.'

11 APRIL, 1890

Joseph Merrick died of asphyxiation in his garret room at the London Hospital, Whitechapel. A truly sensitive and emotional man, he was spurned with horror and abuse most of his life because of the hideous deformities he suffered from an illness (probably proteus syndrome), which saw him cruelly named the 'Elephant Man' by a freak-show proprietor. After making the acquaintance of Dr Frederick Treves, Joseph eventually sought sanctuary at the London Hospital in 1886. Joseph was given a garret room and spent the rest of his life in the only safe 'home' he had ever known. Joseph often read this poem:

Joseph Merrick.

'Tis true my form is something odd,
But blaming me is blaming God;
Could I create myself anew
I would not fail in pleasing you.
If I could reach from pole to pole
Or grasp the ocean with a span
I would be measured by the soul;
The mind's the standard of the man.

12 APRIL, People of the Streets: Toshers

One of the people to be given a wide berth on the street was the tosher. Whole families followed the tosher trade of descent into the gloom of the sprawling sewerage network of London and spent their days sieving excrement and effluvia for the likes of coins, jewellery and silver cutlery which may have been flushed away or lost when a sink was emptied. The foul smell of the effluent in which they worked clung to their clothes, and their houses often stunk too. Marriage into a tosher family was looked down on in the East End. The one real benefit of being a tosher was that the constant exposure to vile substances from early age gave them a far greater immunity to the diseases of the time than that enjoyed by their cleaner neighbours.

13 APRIL, 1888

At Worship Street Court, Patrick Sullivan, a labourer who resided on Fashion Street, Spitalfields, was charged with violently assaulting Esther Hewett. Appearing in the witness box with her head bandaged, Esther described herself as a charwoman. She stated that at 1.00 a.m. on the morning of the assault, she was making her way home to Brick Lane and noticed she was being followed from street to street by the accused. While she was passing through Fashion Street, Sullivan suddenly ran in front of her and knocked her down. He then threw himself upon her, held her by the throat and shook her. Luckily PC 451H observed the incident and rushed over to pull the man off. Sullivan's only defence was that she had hit him first. He was found guilty of assault and was sentenced to six months' imprisonment with hard labour.

14 APRIL, People of the Streets: Jellied-Eel Sellers

The eel-jelly trade was carried on by street stall-sellers 'in all its glory' in the East End. George R. Sims, in *Living London*, described the business thus: 'In great white basins you see a savory mess. Behind the stall mother and father, sometimes assisted by son and daughter, wash up cups and spoons, and ladle out the local luxury to a continuous stream of customers. Many a time on a terribly cold night have I watched a shivering, emaciated-looking man eagerly consuming his cup of eel-jelly and only parting with the spoon and crockery when even the tongue of a dog could not have extracted another drop from either.'

15 APRIL, Life and Death in the Abyss: Mean Streets

Miller's Court, the scene of the most vile of all the Jack the Ripper killings (see 9 November), was just one of a number of cramped yards and courts which ran off Dorset Street (now completely demolished after it was renamed Duval Street). Detective Sergeant Leeson said of this infamous area, 'It was a toss up whether it or Ratcliffe Highway could claim the honour of being London's worst crime street . . . Dorset Street was known to local people as "do as you please" and it quite justified its title.' It was said that many a constable was seen to stop dead from the pursuit of a running suspect if he went down Dorset Street. It was believed locally that if the bobby carried on down the street without reinforcements, he could well have been found beaten to death up some alley – and nobody would have seen a thing! On this street were such characters as 'Mad Jack' O'Brien. Always stripped to the waist and of great physique, he would fight anyone. O'Brien was stood free drinks by landlords to 'op it!' Another was 'Tommy No-Legs', a match seller with two wooden stumps for legs, who would take one of his legs off and smash up the pub with it when he got roaring drunk. Here was also Mrs Flower of the Flock, who carried a knife in her bodice and was not afraid to use it. Policemen thought twice before arresting her when she was drunk.

Street of infamy – Dorset Street, *c.* 1888.

16 APRIL, Prisons and Punishments: Tothill Fields Prison

This prison replaced the old Westminster Bridewell in 1834. Built for 900 prisoners, the numbers within frequently exceeded its intended capacity. By 1850 an undertaking was adopted that Clerkenwell would hold those awaiting trial, Coldbath Fields would take convicted adult males and Tothill Fields would take females and convicted males under 17 years of age. Prisoners picked oakum, knitted, did laundry and made bonnets for the patients in Hanwell Lunatic Asylum. Henry Mayhew wryly observed of the boys' juvenile section in the prison, 'Visiting justices, and Governors and warders, with bunches of keys dangling from thick chains, and strings of cutlasses hanging over the mantelpiece of the entrance office – and all to take care of the little desperate malefactors, not one of whom has cut his "wisdom teeth"; while many are so young that they seem better fitted to be conveyed to the place in a perambulator, than in the lumbering and formidable prison van.' Tothill Fields was finally closed and demolished in 1884. Westminster Catholic Cathedral stands on the foundations laid for the prison. (This is not unique; the Catholic Norwich Cathedral also stands on the site of the old Norwich City Gaol.)

17 APRIL, People of the Streets: Beggars

Physical disability was a very visible and accepted fact of life on the streets of Victorian London. Men and women bent double with malformed spines, rickety-legged beggars on

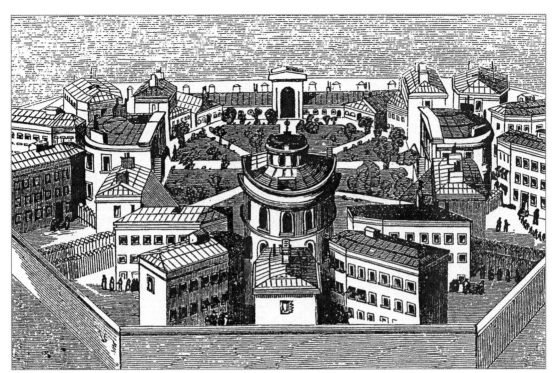

Tothill Fields Prison, *c.* 1875.

crutches, all manner of deformities, amputees, the blind, deaf, dumb or combinations of the aforementioned were all to be found on the streets of London. A number of beggars who were on the streets for many a year became well-known 'characters' and people did look out for them. If they were not at their usual pitch, at least the question why would be asked. One such character had been a shunter at Bricklayer's Arms goods yard in the Old Kent Road who had lost both his legs when he was run over by a goods train. When he was out begging he displayed a crude painting of the incident that showed blood not only spurting out on to the rails in the painting but over the frame too!

18 APRIL, 1887

Thomas William Currell was executed at Newgate for the murder of his sweetheart, Lydia Green, at Horton. Currell asked his sweetheart to marry him and was turned down. The following day, taking with him a revolver he had purchased some time before and seething with venom and anger, he went back to Lydia's family home and obtained entry by borrowing the lodger's key. After cold-bloodedly shooting the woman he claimed to love, he left to go to his father's house, throwing the murder weapon into the Regent's Canal on the way. Currell never seemed to have expressed any regret and even intimated that he repudiated the suggestion he did not know what he was doing when he shot her. He was found guilty, sentenced to death and went resolutely to the gallows. He died instantaneously at the bottom of a drop of 5ft 6in courtesy of public executioner James Berry.

A BUSY CRIPPLE (STROUD GREEN ROAD).

BLIND (REGENT STREET).

BLIND (REGENT STREET).

PARALYSED (VICTORIA STREET).

"MATCHES AND LACES!"

BLIND (ST. MARTIN'S CHURCH STEPS).

CRIPPLED (REGENT STREET).

19 APRIL, People of the Streets: Dockers

Dockers were the men who manhandled the cargo removed from trading vessels to the warehouses on the docks. Anyone desperate for a day's work would await the 'call on' for the day at the dock gates from the early hours of the morning, but the trouble was that there were too many dockers for too few jobs. Literally hundreds would gather at the gates. When they opened the men would swarm in to get a ticket of employment from the contractors, who would assay their potential workers from wooden pulpits. Punches were thrown and kicks exchanged in the scramble for employment. And all this for 5d for a *hard* day's work. On average a docker would take home about 30s a week, but then perhaps be unlucky enough not to work for a fortnight. After two weeks with scarcely a thing to eat, most dockers were too weak to do their manual job properly. In 1889 the dockers went on strike and got better pay and conditions, but the 'casual' system continued into the twentieth century.

Many cargoes were valuable and dockers were regularly searched for pilfered goods.

20 APRIL, Life and Death in the Abyss: Scavenging

Jack London witnessed this incident with his own eyes as he walked up Mile End Road with a carter and a carpenter who had fallen on hard times and were seeking refuge in the workhouse: 'From the slimy, spittle-drenched sidewalk, they were picking up bits of orange peel, apple skin, and grape stems, and they were eating them. . . . They picked up stray crumbs of bread the size of peas, apple cores so black and dirty one would not take them to be apple cores, and these things these two men took into their mouths and chewed them and swallowed them . . . (and all this happened) in the heart of the greatest, wealthiest and most powerful empire the world has ever seen.'

21 APRIL, 1888

The Lea Mystery. On the evening of the 21st, Elizabeth Ann Smith (25) was seen walking with a man described as 'a young toff' in Greyhound Gardens by the River Lea. She was later seen dancing with the man at the nearby Carmen's Rest Coffee House where she was remembered because she had passed out and had to be revived with snuff. She was last spotted leaving a nearby pub and walking up the road in an apparent state of intoxification with two men. She was found drowned a week later in the river. Despite one side of her face and a portion of her hand being consumed by rats, she was positively identified by her father. By the reports of 5 May the men seen with her, George Anthony and Charles Contor, had been traced and were under remand to stand trial. There was no clear evidence of foul play. Anthony and Contor were acquitted and the death of Miss Smith was recorded as a tragic accident.

22 April, 1885

Reports were published of the case brought before Worship Street Court of Thomas Paine (44), a shoemaker of Quinn's Buildings, Russia Lane, Bethnal Green. Paine returned home drunk to the small dwelling filled with his wife, mother-in-law, two children and an elderly visitor. A quarrel erupted as he stumbled around the tiny room, and in a fit of rage he grabbed a saucepan of boiling water from the range and threw it over everyone, scalding all of them to a greater or lesser extent. The children and elderly visitor were still in a dangerous condition when this hearing was held, and the prisoner was remanded until their survival could be assured.

A coachman from the Royal Mews, c. 1888.

24 April, People of the Streets: Cabmen

No bustling street scene of Victorian London was complete without hansom cabs and growlers (although it must be said the streets of Whitechapel only saw such vehicles occasionally). A hansom had two wheels and carried two passengers, whereas a growler (named after the irascibility of many of their drivers) had four wheels and room for four people. Hansoms were not for the nervous as they had no real form of brakes. Their block brakes stopped the cab rolling down a hill, but on the flat only a well-checked horse kept the hansom static. If the horse fell, the fare would be pitched forward out of his seat, and in wet weather, when a glass screen protected the fare, such an accident could result in horrific injuries. Cabs could be hired at 6d an hour (8d when waiting). For specific journeys it was always best to judge the fare by time, such as 15 minutes, which represented a fare of 1s 6d with 2d for luggage.

The clattering and grinding of carriage wheels was such that some hospitals strewed the surrounding streets with straw to deaden the noise, as did private householders if one of the family was ill. It is estimated that there were 300,000 working horses in London in the late nineteenth century and that they created over 450 tons of dung *every day*, which had to be removed from the streets.

25 APRIL, Prisons and Punishments: The Public Executioner

If Jack the Ripper had been caught and found sane enough to stand trial on a capital charge, the man most likely to have sent him on his final journey would have been James Berry, the public executioner 1884–92. A no nonsense Yorkshireman and former policeman on the Wakefield West Riding Constabulary, he was the successor to Executioner William Marwood after his death in 1883. Marwood had applied a technological approach to executions, adopting a table of drops based on height and weight to estimate the correct length or rope needed to dislocate vertebrae in the neck to induce instant death rather than slow strangulation. Berry carried out 131 executions during his incumbency as public executioner. He took three attempts to hang John 'Babbercombe' Lee (on the third attempt intervention was made by the chaplain and Lee's sentence was commuted to life imprisonment) and Robert Goodale's head was torn off by the drop at Norwich Castle in 1885. Berry was not a callous man and it is hardly surprising that he was haunted by these experiences. After resigning as hangman, Berry eventually became an itinerant evangelical preacher.

26 APRIL, 1871

The Eltham murder. Jane Clouson (17) was found, her head horribly injured, in the early hours crawling along Kidbrook Lane, which ran along Eltham Common. She died in Guy's Hospital without giving a clear account of what had happened to her. After the news broke of the crime, some 20,000 were said to have visited the murder site over the ensuing days. Investigations led to Edmund Pook (20), the son of the master of the house where she worked. Earlier in the year it had become known that she was pregnant by the young man and pressure was being put on him to 'make an honest woman of her'. He was due to meet her on Eltham Common on the night she was murdered, and a local shopkeeper even identified the hammer she was attacked with as one he had sold to Pook. However, at his trial Pook's alibi of a romantic assignation with another woman in Greenwich could not be completely disproved, so Pook was acquitted. Public outcry at what many believed was a serious miscarriage of justice came to a head in July when a horse-drawn truck with a tableau of a man bludgeoning a woman to death with a hammer mounted on the back was escorted by 4,000 screaming and shouting supporters to the front of the Pook family residence on Greenwich High Road.

27 APRIL, 1895

Hannah Wilson was brought before Westminster Court charged with having no visible means of support. She claimed to be the daughter of a farmer from the Isle of Man and to have been taken to Edinburgh, and now London, by a man who had deserted her. She seemed generally confused. Correspondence was exchanged with the Isle of Man but no farm she named existed there. The magistrate learned that Wilson had 'led a disreputable life in Sunderland' immediately before she came to London and declared her an 'evidently . . . worthless wandering creature'. She was let go with a warning not to be seen before the magistrates again.

28 APRIL, 1880

An inquest was held at Railway Tavern, Catford, on the body of local horse dealer George Heath (25). It was revealed that the young man had been a teetotaller for several months but was 'of excitable temperament'. On the previous Saturday something had occurred to excite Heath and by the evening he had broken his pledge and was drinking raw spirits and ale in the Black Horse on Rushey Green, Lewisham. Leaving the pub he went to the shop of Mr Read where he bought two separate quarter ounces of opium he said was for his restless mare. Heath was seen entering his father's stable at midnight. George Hepton, his father's stableman, went in to feed the horses on Sunday morning and discovered Heath in an insensible state with an empty opium packet beside him. Mr Steele the surgeon was sent for but Heath died at 1 p.m. in the afternoon. Mr Steele stated that the packet taken by Heath had contained far more than the four grains of opium needed to kill a man. The jury returned a verdict of suicide while labouring under temporary insanity.

29 APRIL, 1882

Dr George Henry Lamson was executed at Wandsworth Gaol. Lamson was an intelligent and adventurous young man who had a promising career ahead of him after qualifying as a doctor in 1874. He had but one real problem, when on one of his adventures in the Balkans, during the Franco-Prussian War, Lamson had developed an addiction to morphine. It affected his work, lost him his practice and consequently caused such financial difficulties that he lived by passing false cheques. Lamson's wife's mother, the widow of a wealthy Manchester merchant, left her fortune in trust to her three sons and two daughters until they were 21. One son, Herbert, was already dead, and in 1879 the second son, Harry, also died from a mysterious stomach complaint. This left Lamson's wife, her sister Margaret and the youngest son, Percy, a cripple. If young Percy was to die, Lamson would inherit over £700 through his wife's interest. Obtaining quinine sulphate powder and one grain of aconite, Lamson set about poisoning his nephew during a family holiday and even when he returned to Blenheim Special School at Wimbledon. After a visit from his uncle, when he gave the lad a slice of Dundee cake, the poor boy finally died. An alkaloid poison was detected in the boy's stomach during post mortem and a raisin removed from the stomach was tested and

The execution of Dr George Henry Lamson.

found to contain aconite. Lamson was concerned that he was not totally absolved of suspicion, so he went personally to Scotland Yard to clear up any misconceptions the police might have. He was not aware that the assistant where he bought the poison had connected his name to the case when he saw the inquest report. Lamson was immediately arrested and sent to Wandsworth. Lamson's trial lasted six days. The jury were left in no doubt of his guilt and passed a guilty verdict after just thirty minutes.

30 APRIL, 1880

An inquest took place before Mr S.F. Langham at the Vestry Room, St Martin's, Strand, on the body of an unknown gentleman found in the Thames off Whitehall Stairs by PC George Collies 144A on the 24th. Dr Mills stated he had conducted a post-mortem and found all organs healthy but the brain and lungs congested. He suggested death had been caused by either apoplexy or drowning. There were no marks of violence on the body, and he was still wearing his gold watch and chain and carrying personal effects. An open verdict was recorded and a description of the man was circulated to the police. On the same day in the evening, Mr Langham held an inquest at Westminster Session House on the body of a woman found dead in the Thames by a waterman named Thomas Newman. About her person were found pawn tickets in the name of Ann Read and Andrews but no further information as to her identity was found despite investigations. An open verdict was recorded. History, in these cases, and like so many at the time, does not record if anyone ever came forward to claim the bodies or reveal if they were connected in any way .

30 APRIL, Prisons and Punishments: The 'Silent System'

The 'separate and silent system' was typical of mid-Victorian prison reform notions, whereby the intention was to transform prisons from the sickness-ridden dank 'holes' of the last 900 years, where convicted felons were simply incarcerated and mixed together with little regard and old lags taught young inmates the ways of crime, to places of

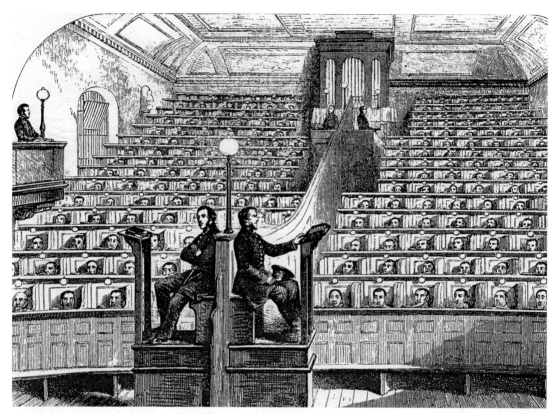

A prison congregation in 'upright coffins' at Pentonville Prison Chapel.

discipline, punishment and education towards 'the straight and narrow' honest life. The 'separate system' was designed so that every prisoner, once admitted to gaol, was kept in solitary confinement and apart from prison officers and officials. When outside of their cells in the exercise yard, the male prisoners wore masks that only allowed the prisoner to see the ground, and women wore veils, so no prisoner could recognise another. Prisoners were exercised in groups with long lengths of chain between them that were not allowed to touch the ground. This ensured that prisoners kept their distance and did not communicate. Prisoners were not allowed visitors. They were to be reformed through solitude to contemplate their wrongs, prayer, work and religious instruction. Even prison chapels had stalls rather than pews for the inmates. The prison chaplain would look out on a congregation in what appeared to be upright coffins! The prisoners looking back would only be able to see the chaplain. If a felon condemned under sentence of death was in the gaol, he would be in the pew directly in front of the pulpit and the only other prisoner visible to the inmates. The 'separate system' was gradually phased out by the late nineteenth century through the increased demands on the space in prisons brought about by the end of transportation and the increasing instances of insanity among prisoners caused by the 'separate system'. Solitary confinement became and still remains as a punishment for misbehaviour by prisoners.

MAY

The central courtyard, Newgate Prison, *c.* 1895. To the left may be seen the
chevaux de frise with male cell-block windows visible above. The gate by which the warder is standing
is part of the old gaol and through here pass the friends and relations of prisoners on visiting day.
Demolished in the early twentieth century, nothing of this mighty and infamous prison remains
today. The Central Criminal Court of the Old Bailey now stands
on the site.

1 MAY 1888

An inquest was held at Manor Rooms, Hackney, before coroner Wynne E. Baxter, into the death of Elizabeth Ann Smith (25). It transpired that her body had been found by Police Sergeant Edward Hatley 20J and PC Yates 295J in the River Lea. The body was searched but no money was found; it was then removed to the mortuary via Hackney Police Station. Evidence given by the deceased's sister and fiancé revealed Elizabeth had gone out drinking alone at the Greyhound. She was discovered by her betrothed at the pub much the worse for drink and they rowed. He slapped her face and left her. She left the Greyhound and was taken into the living quarters of the Carmen's Rest by the daughter of the landlord, Sarah Martin, who saw the poor woman was distressed and ill. Recovering herself Elizabeth left, saying, 'My heart aches, not my head.' She was never seen alive again.

2 MAY 1888

James White (65), a shoemaker of Eden Place, Chelsea, was indicted for the murder of his wife, Margaret, at the Old Bailey. On 3 March Mrs White and her daughter-in-law had been out delivering customers' boots and collecting payments in Balham. She returned with 12s, and Mr White, who smelt of drink, demanded the money to buy more. When he awoke the next day hung over and depressed, he blamed his wife and scolded her for giving him the money. A fight broke out in which he grabbed a poker and struck the life out of her. When people visited the shop later, he was seen to go into the back bedroom with the poker and deliver some more blows to her body with it. Police were summoned and he was taken into custody. Resigned to his fate, he said, 'I suppose the Old Bailey will be my lot.' At his trial he was found guilty but with a strong recommendation for mercy on account of his age and mental state. His death sentence was commuted to imprisonment.

3 MAY 1899

Frederick James Andrews (45) was executed at Wandsworth. Andrews lived with Frances Short in a small lodging house in Kensington. Andrews was a heavy drinker who regularly beat Frances and sent her out to keep him in beer by selling fruit and vegetables from a stall. In one of his drunken moods he decided to take his anger out on Frances again, but she could take no more and threatened to leave. Andrews grabbed his pocket-knife, cut her throat and stabbed her over forty times. He then pawned her clothes and went drinking. Soon arrested, he stood trial and was found guilty. He was sentenced to death and executed by James and Thomas Billington.

4 MAY Prisons and Punishments: The Lash

While the birch was mostly a corporal punishment for wayward boys, adult males who took the path of crimes against the person, such as robbery with violence, and especially garotting (see 22 February, p. 37), would receive 'the lash'. The *Illustrated Police News* related the following after witnessing this punishment at Newgate in 1871: 'The effects on his skin were horrible, the diagonal pink lines glowing scarlet and running into one another till there was a broad scarlet band which quivered and flushed and changed colour, but there was no blood. Twenty-four, twenty-five lashes and then came a loud voice "Stop" and the prisoner was cut loose to walk quietly away from the post.'

5 MAY People of the Streets: Swallowers

One of the most common 'entertainers' was the swallower. Going beyond the stage trickery of the sword swallowers, these men, often dressed in clothes no more fancy than those of an East End working man, carried with them small tables or stands covered in plush material trimmed with gold tassels. On this well-presented surface were placed the objects the entertainer would swallow if a suitable offering was collected from his audience. Interspersed with jokes, and building up a peak of anticipation, the man then swallowed one of the items on display, be it a piece of glass, pebbles, nails, tacks or a similar delicacy. So numerous were these entertainers that one commentator suggested that such a diet was quite nourishing!

6 MAY 1888

Thomas Shannon (22), described as a newsvendor living in Tenpenny's Lodging House, Widegate Street, City, was charged at Worship Street Court with selling a certain publication entitled *Town Talk*. This publication was deemed 'indecent', and eighteen copies of it were produced in evidence. When asked by Mr Bushby, the magistrate, what he thought he was doing, Shannon replied, 'I didn't know I was doing any harm.' He also claimed the paper was in wide circulation and that the printers should be charged and not himself. Shannon was fined 10s and the remaining copies were destroyed.

7 MAY 1889

Eliza Kingsbury (41), a married woman of 122 Rhodeswell Road, Limehouse, appeared at Thames Police Court charged on remand for attempting to take her own life and that of her son George (5 months) by drowning themselves in Regent's Canal. Mrs Kingsbury had been discovered with her feet in the canal and the babe in her arms, and when challenged she exclaimed, 'Let me drown myself. Mine is a miserable, unhappy home. I am a miserable woman.' The babe was taken from her with difficulty for she appeared to be 'seized with a fit', and they removed her to the police station. Investigations revealed she had previously attempted to take her life with poison. In court Eliza stated she had no intention of murder or suicide. She had 'got in a temper', and when she had cooled down she intended to go home. She was committed to appear at the Central Criminal Court.

8 MAY 1889

Henry Green (50), a labourer, pleaded guilty at the Central Criminal Court to three indictments of burglary at Wandsworth. A number of previous convictions were considered and Green was sent down for eight years. Events were keenly watched by Mr Peace, a concerned citizen who asked that representations be made to Scotland Yard that an order by the late Metropolitan Police Commissioner, Sir Charles Warren, forbidding the police to examine the backs of premises be withdrawn after a spate of rear entry burglaries at Dulwich.

9 MAY 1879

An errand boy, William Strohman, who had been sent to clear out the cellar of the Bastendorff residence in Euston Square, discovered the decomposing body of a woman wrapped in cloth with a rope tied round her neck. The body was identified by Edmund Hacker, who stated it was his unmarried sister Matilda, an eccentric woman who had been missing for some months. The previous occupant of the Euston Square residence, who had left without giving notice about six months previously, was a Miss Uish. Inquiries revealed that Miss Uish's servant, Hannah Dobbs, was thought to be in possession of some of Miss Hacker's trinkets. Dobbs was traced, arrested and tried but was not convicted of any crime. She wrote a book on the affair, attacking her former master, who, after bringing an action for libel, was convicted of perjury. The murder of Miss Hacker and quite where Miss Uish disappeared to remain unsolved.

10 MAY 1889

George Hare, a man who described himself as a herbalist of Portobello Road, and his housekeeper Lillian Ayliffe appeared before the Central Criminal Court. Not to put too fine a point on it, Hare and Ayliffe were backstreet abortionists. They stood accused of two cases of conducting operations 'with an instrument with intent to procure a miscarriage' by which means Elizabeth Louisa Davies had been seriously injured and Rhoda Fayers met her death. Found guilty, Ayliffe, the assistant, received five years and Hare ten.

11 MAY 1888

Charles Price (25) appeared before Worship Street Court charged with having stolen 5d by picking the pocket of Mrs Moses Morris of Whitechapel. She had been unaware that her pocket had been picked until it was pointed out to her by a witness who identified Price as the pickpocket. PC Fluister attested that the accused had een convicted of felony in 1886. Mr Bushby, the magistrate, then committed the prisoner to trial.

12 MAY 1888

Joseph Berger (29) and Mike Paster (18) appeared at Thames Police Court charged with 'exposing indecent photos for sale' on barrows on the Whitechapel Road. Arrested by Inspector Reid of H Division, Berger was found to be offering 173 indecent photos and Paster 83. Berger was fined 40s and Paster 20s or one month's imprisonment for default. The photos were destroyed upon application of Inspector Reid.

13 MAY 1900

Alfred Highfield (22) and Edith Poole (19) had been seeing each other for over six years and had set a wedding date for August 1900. Things began to go wrong when Alf blamed Edie for losing him his job at the Westminster Brewery Company; they rowed and she refused to see him. He remained on good terms with Edie's family, and it was engineered that they should both come round for Easter tea. After the meal everyone went out for a walk. Edie and Alf held back from the group and talked and there were great hopes for a reconciliation. Suddenly there was a cry and the group turned to see Alf kneeling over the prostrate Edie. Her brother rushed over and pulled Alf off, and to his horror saw his sister's throat had been cut with a razor. Taken into custody, Highfield said, 'I know what I have done. I don't care if I die for it.' Despite him pleading manslaughter at his trial on the grounds that he was provoked, and that they struggled and he cut her throat by mistake, the jury eventually returned a verdict of guilty. Highfield was executed at Newgate by James Billington on 17 July 1900.

14 MAY 1898

William Ewart Gladstone (1809–1898), Prime Minister and great Victorian statesman died on this day. He was rabidly against Irish Catholics and liked to be known for his strong morals. He was responsible for the Licensing Act of 1870 which made gin so expensive that many turned to opium. It was also no doubt in the course of his 'moral crusade' that he was regularly spotted in the areas of London notorious for their prostitution. When Gladstone felt he deserved chastisement, he flagellated himself with his own cat o' nine tails and marked the event by drawing a small whip in his journal; the number of straps on the whip denoted the number of lashes he had inflicted on himself.

William Ewart Gladstone.

A group of London prison warders, *c.* 1880.

15 MAY Prisons and Punishments: Millbank

Millbank Penitentiary was, for the majority of the nineteenth century, a gaunt and ominous-looking penal colony on the bank of the Thames near Pimlico. Opened in 1816, it was built of yellow-brown brick and was even surrounded on the landward side by a moat. A huge prison, Millbank was designed with single cells for 1,000 prisoners to maintain the 'separate system' (see 30 April) and was specifically aimed at reforming inmates. Work was arduous but not pointless like the treadmill and prisoners were paid for their toils. Some were even allowed to work overtime and amounts in the region of £17 for three months' work were common among inmates by the 1840s. This said, Millbank was a far from pleasant place to stay. The walls were damp and cold and disease spread rapidly here. Scurvy and cholera swept through the prison in 1822 and 1823. When Pentonville opened in 1842, Millbank was downgraded to a convict clearing depot where prisoners were assessed before transfer to other detention centres, and at that time over 4,000 prisoners passed through Millbank each year. In 1870 Millbank became a military prison. It closed in 1890 and was demolished in 1903. The Tate Gallery now occupies the site.

16 MAY 1888

The Canonbury Murder. Two men were observed walking up the steps, knocking and being let in to 19 Canonbury Terrace, Islington, by Mrs Wright, the elderly lady of the house. Soon screams were heard from the premises and her neighbour Madame Chefdeville went to investigate. She received no reply and went to see other neighbours, but they had heard nothing. Returning to the front door, she knocked and was about to raise the alarm when two men walked calmly out. Madame Chefdeville cried 'Burglar' and the men ran off. Poor Mrs Wright was found dead from a blow to the head behind the street door. The opening paragraph of ensuing coverage in the *Penny Illustrated Paper* included the statement, 'London residents cannot be too strongly reminded that there are wild beasts in human form about ever seeking prey . . .' Even they could not imagine the events of the autumn in the same year.

17 MAY 1888

At Worship Street Magistrates Court, George Frederick Weige, John Piggott of Bethnal Green and William Hows of Shoreditch were fined the sums of £10, £8 and £8 respectively for diluting beer and spirits. At the same sessions John Weeden was found guilty of selling mustard adulterated with turmeric (fined £8) and Francis Booth Milner fined £8 plus costs for selling adulterated pepper. Food adulteration was a common crime in London and could be inflicted on a vast array of groceries and drinks from bread, flour and coffee to milk and beer. This crime was truly despised as the goods affected constituted the basic necessities for the poorest people. The feeling was summed up in this popular ditty:

> Little drops of water added to the milk
> Make the milkman's daughter clothe herself in silk.
> Little grains of sand in the sugar mixed
> Make the grocery man soon become well fixed.
> Little acts of meanness, little tricks of trade,
> All pass for keenness, fortunes thus are made.

A council inspector checks a sample from the milk cart.

18 MAY People of the Streets: Dancing Bear Men

One of the most tragic entertainments on the streets was the dancing bear. Most were kept by Italians and Spaniards in miserable dark cellars overnight, fed on bread, sugar, water and scraps and pulled round the streets on a chain to entertain any audience they could draw by day. Their lumbering dance or contrived movement normally drew but a few coppers. Accidents were rare but many a crowd had an extra show if the bear was startled by a sudden noise, like the movement of a boisterous dog. The bear would drop to all fours and bare its teeth, making to retaliate, and it would take all the skills of his master to bring him under control again.

19 MAY 1880

The head of a child was discovered in the Thames. Over the following days further remains were recovered and an inquest was held by Mr G.H. Hull at the Star and Garter, Battersea. Dr William Henry Kempster stated he had examined the remains and concluded that death had occurred about three days previously and that the body 'had been cut up in an unscientific manner'. The inquest was adjourned to enable the police to obtain some clue to the identification of the remains.

20 MAY 1880

An inquest was held at St Pancras Coroner's Court, King's Road, Camden Town, on the body of Joseph Essex (9), who drowned in Regent's Canal the preceding Thursday. It emerged that the boy had gone with his brother, Samuel (10), for a walk along the towpath near Albert Bridge when he overbalanced and fell into the water. Samuel attempted to help his brother but also fell in. Their screams brought a young man named David Sadder to the spot. Sadder dived in the water, pulled out Samuel and was attempting to extricate Joseph when a barge approached. It was called to stop but continued on. Sadder had to get out of the water and the barge passed over the spot where Joseph went down. Sadder leapt in again but two more barges came and refused to stop despite calls from the crowd and freshly arrived police. Sadder, fearful for his own life, climbed out again. Sometime later the body of the boy was dragged from the water. It was evident the barges had driven the body of the poor lad deep into the mud on the bottom of the canal. A Mr Hunt deposed at the inquest that the reason why the bargemen would not stop was because they would receive nothing for their trouble, whereas if they recovered a dead body they received 5s from the county! A verdict of accidental death was recorded, the bargemen were slammed for their 'disgraceful conduct' and a collection was made for Sadder for his gallant rescue efforts.

21 MAY Prisons and Punishments: Hard Labour

This was a familiar addition to sentences like manslaughter or for crimes which carried short sentences but merited extra punishment, such as aggravated theft, brawling or repeat offenders. Typical types of hard labour were the Crank (see 3 December, p. 180), the Treadmill (see 24 June, p. 97), Shot Drill and Stone-Breaking. Shot drill entailed a prisoner having to lift single cannonballs (weighing up to 14.5kg) up to chest height, to carry them a set distance and make another pile, repeating the process until the set number of cannonballs had been moved in like manner. In the larger prisons up to fifty convicts could be engaged in 'shot drill'. They would be formed into three sides of a square and standing three deep and three yards distant from each other. Each end of the open square would have a neat pile of cannonballs that would be picked up one at a time and passed from man to man and from one end to the other. The exercise would be repeated for a standard hour and a quarter. Stone breaking was particularly favoured in the prisons near quarries like Dartmoor or Portland. This soul-destroying task saw the convict smash a set number or weight of stones with a sledge hammer until the boulder was reduced to such a fine gravel it would pass through the sieves monitored by the prison warders.

22 MAY 1900

First man hanged in the twentieth century – for the sake of a shilling. Henry Grove (26) was one of a number of local hawkers who used his neighbour Henry Smith's yard and stables in Enfield for 6d a week. Smith (34) told Grove, who was two weeks behind with the rent, he could not use the stabling again until he had settled his arrears. Grove returned to the yard later that night very drunk and was told where to go by Smith. A row developed and Grove punched Smith, but that was not the end of it. Smith went back into the yard, picked up two rusty scythes and took them to his own garden. Returning a few minutes later Grove followed Smith and battered him to death's door with one of the scythes. Mrs Smith tried to intervene but was fought off by Grove. Mr Smith was removed to hospital and was later able to give a statement to a magistrate in Grove's presence. Smith died of his injuries a few weeks later. At his trial Grove swore he used no weapons, that he did not throw the first punch and was acting in self-defence. The jury were not impressed and returned a guilty verdict. Henry Grove has the infamous distinction of being the first man hanged in the twentieth century.

23 May 1892

Frederick Bailey Deeming was executed on this day. Deeming was a muscular, hard-faced but handsome man, and by all accounts an unusual character. He had travelled throughout the Continent, India, America, Australia and New Zealand and had even worked in the gold fields of South Africa. Always flamboyantly dressed and supremely confident, he carried off such impostures as posing as a Lord Dunn or as an HM Inspector of Regiments. He was also known to those who knew the real Frederick Deeming as 'Mad Fred'. He had committed minor crimes throughout his travels, such as theft and embezzlements, but had always managed to evade prosecution. Deeming married an English girl and had four children by her – all of whom he left destitute in Australia. In 1890 he was back on his home territory of Merseyside and rented a villa from a Mrs Mather. He charmed her, and was soon, having given the impression he was a wealthy and well-connected single man, courting Mrs Mather's pretty daughter, Emily. Mrs Deeming then turned up with the four children. Deeming killed his wife and children with a pickaxe and buried them under the floor of the villa. Deeming and Emily Mather were soon married and on their way to Australia – on alleged HM Inspector business. Within a few days of landing at Melbourne Emily was killed and buried under the floor of their rented house. This time the flooring was left uneven and when the new occupant had it relaid Emily's body was discovered. Deeming stood trial at Melbourne and much was made of his mental state caused by advanced VD. It was said he went out hunting at night for the woman who gave it to him because 'he believed in the extermination of such women'. He was found guilty, and the story got out that he had confessed in the condemned cell to the Ripper killings of Liz Stride and Kate Eddowes. Deeming was executed in front of a crowd of some 10,000 – he contemptuously smoked a cigar as he mounted the scaffold. A cast of his head was taken after his execution and one of the castings found its way to the Black Museum in London where for many years the curator would indicate that this was 'the death mask of Jack the Ripper'. It has been proved that Deeming was, in fact, in South Africa during the 'Autumn of Terror'.

Frederick Bailey Deeming.

24 MAY People of the Streets: Frederick Charrington

One of the most unlikely philanthropists of the East End was Frederick N. Charrington. After a privileged and well-educated upbringing Charrington was keen to step into the fold of his family's famous brewing business at their Mile End Brewery. Inspired by evangelism, he found he had a talent for getting the Christian message across to even 'tough young roughs'. He took to nocturnal wanderings in the East End and was shocked to see, first hand, the ruin caused by his family business pubs. Charrington immediately set about creating a mission shelter for girls in distress in Stepney and soon took his Christian mission on to the streets in a campaign against sin and gin palaces. He carried a large sandwich board with the message 'THE WAGES OF SIN IS DEATH' emblazoned upon it. If he saw a drunk pick up a prostitute, he would go over to them and implore them to reconsider their actions and follow the Christian path. His message was sometimes wasted on very closed ears and he would have to be extricated from a hail of punches by the local constabulary. By 1888 Charrington had been instrumental in the closure of over 200 brothels, rehoming the girls in his own refuge or in the converted mansion which had been left to him by Lady Ashburton.

25 MAY 1874

James Godwin (27), a hearthrug maker, was executed at Newgate for the murder of his wife Louisa at their rooms at 181 Kingsland Road. They had been moving furniture when one of their regular arguments erupted. This time Godwin lost control and struck his wife with a bedpost. Godwin then left the house. Sarah Wilson, a neighbour, was concerned at the noises she had heard and went into the Godwins' room. She discovered Louisa Godwin lying on the floor, covered by a sheet. She was almost insensible and bleeding profusely from her head (despite medical attention she died that night). Wilson summoned a constable. Godwin confessed, was taken into custody, pleaded guilty at his trial and went quietly to the gallows. This execution was also significant because it was to be Calcraft's last, the authorities of London and Middlesex having decided he was too old for the job and should be pensioned off. Godwin was executed in the typical tradition of Calcraft and 'died hard', being hanged and strangled rather than given a decent drop to dislocate the vertebrae.

26 MAY 1897

The publication of Dracula by Bram Stoker. This book was truly the epitome of Gothic horror: an evil foreign count turns out not only to be undead but a drinker of blood, a vampire, a Prince of Darkness who comes to England to stalk the fresh blood of innocent young ladies. The *Pall Mall Gazette* summed up the majority of the reviews by saying, 'It is horrid and creepy to the last degree!' Stoker was a tall and robust Irishman who was employed by his hero Sir Henry Irving, the greatest actor of his day, at his Lyceum Theatre as stage manager. For Ripper conspiracy theorists there is a feast to be had here. When Buffalo Bill Cody came to London he was to be frequently seen deep in discussion with Irving and Stoker as they were driven around Hyde Park in an open

Bram Stoker.

Sir Thomas Hall Caine.

Sir Henry Irving.

carriage. One can but wonder at the content of their conversations; there was without doubt great discussion of Native American Indian methods in stalking and killing their prey. Few realise it was also at the Lyceum that the American actor Richard Mansfield staged his adaptation of *Dr Jekyll and Mr Hyde* in 1888. His stage performance of the transformation from the mild doctor into evil Mr Hyde shocked audiences to such a degree that it was thought he could have inspired Jack the Ripper; consequently the run of the play was brought to an early end (see 27 October, p. 160). If that is not enough it is well known that Stoker was a friend of Sir Thomas Hall Caine, one of the late nineteenth century's most popular authors. The mysterious 'Hommy Beg' to whom the novel *Dracula* is dedicated is none other than Caine, Hommy Beg being the affectionate name given to Caine by his Manx grandmother. In turn Caine has become entwined with the Ripper mystery through his known homosexual relationship with Dr Francis Tumblety, the Ripper suspect named by DCI John George Littlechild (see 24 November, p. 176).

27 MAY People of the Streets: Hokey-Pokey Men or Ice-Cream Johnnies

These ice-cream sellers were made distinctive by gaudily painted hand carts, fine boaters and big moustaches. The ice-cream trade was exclusively in the hands of the Italians. Most of them were Sicilians who were tightly bound into exclusive mafia-like societies with heads known as padrones. Each of these men had a strictly delineated area for which he was responsible. No vendor could set up on his own account – the society saw to that. Each Johnnie would hire his cart from the padrone and set up on his allocated pitch. There were two types of mix on offer, ice-cream and water-ice. Two sizes of thick-stemmed and cupped 'hokey-pokey' (which comes from the Italian *ecco uno poco*, or 'here's a little') glasses were offered. The largest was a penny, the smaller a halfpenny. The most popular call was for a 'topper up of mixed', which was a pennyworth of cream and iced water mixed. Hard-up children could also ask for a 'taster', which was a small wipe of ice-cream on a small tin spoon kept for that purpose. The hygienic arrangements consisted of a bucket of water to wash the hokey-pokey glasses, which were then wiped with a dirty wet cloth. By the end of the day the water looked like creamy pea soup. It is sobering to note that milk and especially the water the ices was made from was one of the main carriers of disease in the nineteenth century; hence the rhyme 'Hokey-Pokey, penny a lick, lick too much and you're dead as a stick.'

28 MAY 1892

Chief Inspector Frederick Abberline, the officer who led the Ripper investigation 'at ground level' in Whitechapel, retires and a few of his reminiscences are recorded to mark the occasion in *Cassell's Saturday Journal* on this day. He sums up his views on the Ripper murders with 'we were lost almost in theories; there were so many of them'. In 1903 Abberline recorded his own theory for the first time in the *Pall Mall Gazette*. George Chapman (a.k.a. Severin Klosowski), 'The Borough Poisoner', was under sentence of death at the time, and when the reporter called on Abberline, he was found to be about to write to Metropolitan Police Commissioner Sir Melville Macnaghten 'to say how strongly I was impressed with the opinion that "Chapman" was also the author of the Whitechapel murders'. Abberline passed the conclusions he had intended to send to Macnaghten directly to the reporter. They outlined the coincidences that pointed to Chapman, especially how the murders had continued in

Chief Inspector Frederick Abberline.

America (Chapman had emigrated to New Jersey in 1891), Chapman's movements and how struck he was with the degree to which Chapman fitted the descriptions they had of the Ripper at the time. Sadly, most of Abberline's thoughts about Chapman as the Ripper do not withstand close scrutiny. Chapman was certainly a killer but he was a poisoner and probably not Jack the Ripper, but if it gave Abberline peace of mind in his declining years that his old comrade Detective Sergeant Godley had been the man to catch Jack the Ripper, who are we to judge?

29 MAY 1888

Charles Whitbread (22), a private soldier in the 7th Battalion, the Rifle Brigade, and James Wimpory (29), a carman, appeared at Worship Street Court charged with assaults on the police. Whitbread had been ejected from a pub and started a fight, in consequence of which Inspector Burnett of G Division apprehended him. Erupting into a rage like a madman, he struck Inspector Burnett in the chest and Burnett struck back, blackening Whitbread's eye; they both fell to the floor grappling. A man named Wimpory went to assist Whitbread and struck Constable 324G. Whitbread continued a desperate resistance and a man named Wastaby who attempted to assist the inspector had his hand bitten in nine places. The inspector received more than one kick in the incident, his knee was injured and head cut open. He was still too ill to give evidence in court. Wimpory was discharged with a warning and Whitbread was sent down with three months with hard labour.

Scotland Yard after the bombing on 30 May 1884.

30 MAY 1884

Scotland Yard bombed. Shortly before 9 p.m. a bomb planted by Fenians tore through the gable end of the CID and Special Irish branch head-quarters in Great Scotland Yard, leaving a 30ft high hole. Luckily no one was injured but the damage to the reputation of the police, having had a bomb go off literally under their noses, was inestimable. Matters were compounded by other bombs being exploded at the Junior Carlton Club and outside Sir Watkin-Wynne's house; there was even an unexploded device found at the foot of Nelson's Column. Fortunately, the fuse attached to the sixteen sticks of dynamite, which would almost certainly have brought the great monument down, was defective.

31 MAY 1886

Henry Selfe (65), a baker, appeared at Westminister Court after being arrested on Buckingham Palace Road. He was so drunk and his offensive language against the Queen and the Prince of Wales was such that he was taken into custody in the belief he was 'a wandering lunatic not under proper control'. In court he strenuously denied the charges and complained bitterly of the treatment he received at the hands of the police. He was remanded pending enquiries into his sanity.

JUNE

✝

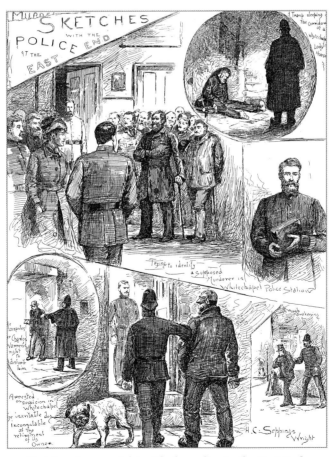

Sketches from a night with the police in the East End,
Illustrated London News, 1888.

1 JUNE People of the Streets: Twisterers and Carpet Acrobats

Acrobats were often thought of as a better class of street performer because many of them were men who had had other careers before being forced to demonstrate their prowess on the street. They would announce their performance with a flourish by laying a fine carpet out on the street. Twisterers, both male and female, were people with such supple and 'double-jointed' bodies they could lie face-down, smiling at the crowd, bring their legs over their back and put their feet beside their ears; some then circled their feet right round their body in a circular motion. In the climax of another act, a man literally folded himself up into an unfeasibly small box and shut the lid!

2 JUNE Life and Death in the Abyss: The Whitechapel Workhouse Infirmary

The greatest fear of people who became too ill or old to work was to end up in the Whitechapel Workhouse Infirmary. Such a fate was viewed with shame by even the poorest people of the East End. Stories circulated, and were firmly believed, that if an inmate patient became too much trouble or was lingering on the edge of death, they would be helped on their way and a much-needed bed freed with a swift dose of 'white potion' or 'blackjack', fatal medicines allegedly administered by the infirmary doctor.

3 JUNE 1880

A body was discovered crammed into an American barrel and covered in chloride of lime (no doubt in the mistaken belief that this chemical would hasten decomposition) in the cellar of 139 Harley Street, London, the home of Jacob Quixona Henriques. Mr Henriques had lived at his Harley Street address for over twenty years and was astonished by the discovery. Despite evidence presented by the three butlers he had engaged over the years no further light could be shed on how the barrel got there, how long it had been there or its occupant. The body discovered was that of a woman about 40 years old. She was almost naked except for the remains of stockings and garters on her legs and her hair appeared to have been cut off. Dr Pepper of St Mary's Hospital stated that she had been stabbed in the chest 'by such as a table knife'. A verdict of murder by person or persons unknown was recorded. The mystery remains unsolved to this day (see also 9 May, p. 78).

4 JUNE 1889

Reports were published of Philip Michaels (21), George McLeod (20) and Reuben Michalls (26), who appeared at Thames Police Court on charges of riotous conduct and fighting in Romford Street, Mile End. Michalls was also charged with damaging two windows owned by Joseph Davey and assaulting the said man by striking him on the head with a revolver. William Beaver (22) and Joseph Garcia (20) were also charged with being involved in riotous conduct. Beaver was also charged with assaulting PC 470H with a stick, and cutting and wounding William McDonald. Moss Michaels was also charged with breaking two windows and assaulting William Davis with a poker in the same incident. The events had arisen when two men passing the Bell Club saw ten men rush out of the building and 'brutally ill-use two women who happened to be passing'. The two men defended the women after which about fifty men from the club followed the men to Romford Street and assaulted them. Sentences were swift and hard. Beaver was given four months with hard labour for his assault on the constable plus two months' hard labour for assaulting McDonald, Cohen received two months' hard labour for assault and was bound over. Reuben received two months' hard labour for assault and was bound over. Michalls received seven weeks' hard labour for assault and all others were bound over on sureties of £100 or spend a month in gaol.

5 June 1888

James Cannon (37), a labourer, of Jacob Street, Bethnal Green appeared at Worship Street Court charged with assaulting his wife Emma by kicking her in the head for being drunk. Cannon had been in custody for over three weeks because his wife would not appear against him and she had to be brought to court under a warrant. Mrs Cannon had been taken to hospital and Mr Cannon was taken into custody – he even admitted he had kicked his wife to the arresting constable. When standing in the dock Emma Cannon could not bring herself to testify against her husband. The magistrate asked if she would like a judicial separation to which she replied, 'No, he's not been a bad husband to me.' Cannon said he had nothing to say on the matter so he was sentenced to six months with hard labour under the evidence gathered by the police.

6 June 1889

A report was published of the inquest on the body of Caroline Chivers (19) at the Effra Hall Tavern, Brixton. Chivers and a friend named Joseph Goodsall, journeyman butcher, were playing with loaded revolvers, one of which Goodsall fired with fatal results as the bullet passed through Caroline's right eye and lacerated her brain. Goodsall had been arrested but the jury were satisfied there was no malicious intent and passed a verdict of accidental death.

7 June 1890

Policemen disgruntled by a lack of proper pension provision and pay scales, and desirous of starting a union came out on strike at Bow Street. Joined by socialist activists and an unruly mob of 'supporters', they threatened to knock down any man seen going on duty at Bow Street, marched up and down the street singing 'Rule Britannia' and then hung around the area armed with flour bombs and rotten vegetables; these they hurled at the mounted police officers when they arrived to control the situation. The strike ended when Assistant Commissioner Howard invited the policemen on the station steps to come in and discuss their grievances. The mob was dowsed with a bowl of water from the upper windows of the police station and were already dispersing as two troops of Life Guards trotted into Bow Street.

8 JUNE 1889

The case of Winnifred Trimlett (13) was reported, who decoyed Florence Prendergast away from her parents and wandered about stealing from other children and cemeteries, and sleeping rough with the little girl for the next four days. It transpired that Trimlett had abducted children before and stolen items of their clothing. Trimlett was found guilty and sent to industrial school.

9 JUNE 1870

Charles Dickens died at Gad's Hill Place. Over the last thirty years of his life Dickens had observed and moved within every strata of Victorian society from slums, workhouses and prisons to state rooms, mansions and royalty. His books, marked by their attention to human details and foibles, keen social observation, humour and realism, provide a canon of works that are invaluable not only for their literary value, but the social history he records on the pages of such classic volumes as *Oliver Twist* (1838), *David Copperfield* (1850), *Bleak House* (1853) and *Great Expectations* (1861). Dickens made his last public appearance to deliver one of his famous readings at St James's Hall (now the Piccadilly Hotel) on 15 March 1870.

10 JUNE 1896

Mrs Amelia Dyer (57), baby farmer, was executed at Newgate. Although executed in London, Dyer, like most baby farmers, had operated at several locations across Britain and in her case had done so quite successfully for about fifteen years. Living at 45, Kensington Road, Reading, at the time of her capture, she was traced there after a baby wrapped in brown paper was pulled out of the water at Caversham Lock by a bargeman. The infant had been strangled by a piece of fabric tape. Dyer had made a fatal mistake: she had wrapped the baby in paper from a parcel sent to her at her old address of 20 Pigott's (spelt Wigott's on the parcel) Road, Caversham. She had also been spotted by a witness before the horrible discovery waddling up the Caversham towpath with a parcel under her arm. By the time the police came knocking at her door, a total of seven babies had been recovered from the Thames, and Lord knows how many were never found. Shortly after Dyer's arrest, her daughter and son-in-law – Polly and Arthur Palmer – were arrested at their Willesden home. More baby clothes were found there. Their complicity in Dyer's horrible trade seemed clear but there was no evidence to link them to any crime. Young Polly made every effort to deflect any blame and condemnation on to her mother. The Palmers were acquitted but Mrs Dyer went to the gallows. Chillingly, when Mrs Dyer was asked about the identification of the babies, she replied, 'You'll know mine by the tape around their necks.' The ice-cold glower of Mrs Dyer frightened generations of visitors to Madame Tussaud's Waxworks.

11 JUNE 1890

Reports appeared in the press of the previous day's execution at Wandsworth of Daniel Stewart Gorrie (30) for the murder of Thomas Furlonger. Both men were employed as bakers at Nevill's Bakery in Herne Hill. In the evening the elderly Mr Furlonger picked up his week's wages of 22s; he was battered to death with an iron bar on his way home. Gorrie had been seen in the vicinity of the crime, and when asked to turn out his pockets by the police, he was carrying far more money than he could possibly have earned. Gorrie asserted his innocence to the end, when he kept an appointment with public executioner James Berry.

12 JUNE 1886

Daniel Dunglas Home died on this day. Home was truly a spiritualist phenomenon. He is thought to have conducted about 1,500 seances in front of audiences which included gentry, magicians, scientists, priests and policemen, and no trace of trickery was ever attributed to him. On one occasion he was seen to float out of a third-floor window of Ashley House and returned to his audience via another. Home died of TB and was buried at St Germain-en-Laye.

13 JUNE 1892

Sioux Indian Chief Long Wolf (59) was buried at Brompton Cemetery. This great Indian chief had died of bronchial pneumonia while appearing with Buffalo Bill's Wild West Show at Earl's Court during its European tour. Long Wolf's dying wish was to be returned home to his native soil for burial, but his wife feared he would be put over the side of the ship and buried at sea. Buffalo Bill Cody therefore saw to it that a respectful burial was made and fine stone memorial set up. The story did not end there. Over 100 years later, Elizabeth Knight, a Worcestershire housewife, was so moved to read that Long Wolf's grave was laying overgrown and forgotten she set about tracing his living family and raising the money to have the great chief returned home. With due ceremony and reverence Long Wolf was exhumed and returned home for interment at the Oglala Sioux burial ground at the Pine Ridge Reservation in September 1997.

'Buffalo Bill' Cody.

Memorial cross erected on the grave of Chief Long Wolf at Brompton Cemetery.

14 JUNE 1889

Thomas (who described himself as a billiard-cue maker) and Ruth Jones appeared before Marlborough Street Court charged with keeping part of their house on Archer Street, St James's, as a brothel. Found guilty they were fined £5 each with Mr Jones ordered to pay two guineas costs or suffer one month's imprisonment in default.

15 JUNE Prisons and Punishments: Surrey County Gaol

This prison on Horsemonger Lane was constructed between 1791 and 1798. Known initially as the 'New Gaol', it was built with accommodation for 400 prisoners. Public executions were carried out on the roof of the gaol above the main gate. Crowds would come in their thousands to observe the proceedings, especially if the criminal going to his doom had acquired notoriety. The infamous criminals that hanged here include the conspirator and traitor Colonel Despard in 1803 and Mr and Mrs Manning, who murdered their lodger in 1849. Charles Dickens was present among the crowd at this latter execution. He was deeply affected by the scene and wrote, 'I do not believe that any community can prosper where such a scene of horror as was enacted this morning outside Horsemonger Lane is permitted.' His voice was just one of an increasing body which demanded the end of public executions. They were

Exterior of Horsemonger Lane Gaol, c. 1875.

A. Infirmary.
B. Boys' Cells.
C. Laundry.
D. Women's Baths.
E. Women's Side.
F. Visitors' Room.

G. Boys' Airing Yard.
H. Women's Airing Yard.
I. Kitchen, etc.
J. Female Debtors' Yard.
K. Offices.
L. Governor's House.

M. Chapel.
N. School-room.
O. Cells.
P. Men's Airing Yard.
Q. Court.
S. Master Debtors.

T. Men's Baths.
U. Female Debtors.
V. Common Debtors.
W. Men's Side.
X. Airing Courts.
Y. Sessions House.

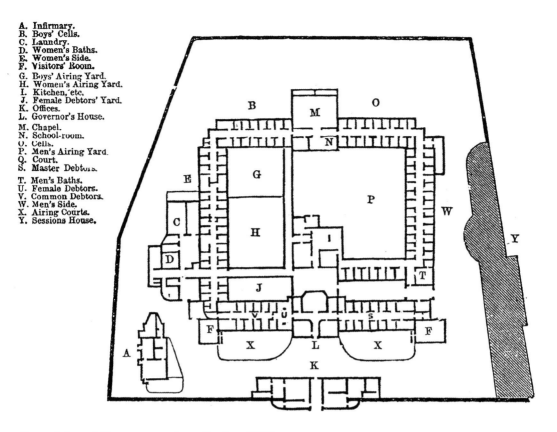

Groundplan of Horsemonger Lane Gaol, *c.* 1875.

banned by law in 1868 but the ultimate judicial sentence was still carried out within prisons, and Horsemonger Lane was no exception. The last execution to be carried out at Horsemonger Lane was that of Margaret Walters, the baby farmer, on 11 October 1870 (see 11 October, p. 155). Horsemonger Lane was finally closed by the prison commissioners in 1878. The site is now a public park on the south side of Harper Road and east of Newington Causeway. Local children still say they are going to play in 'the gaol'!

16 JUNE 1889

William Young, an old man recently released from a long prison sentence, was seen on Hill Road, Wimbledon, making great effort of carrying a basket concealed under his apron. When challenged by a passing police sergeant, the old lag revealed its contents to be an assortment of tools, saying, 'You had better take them to the station . . . I stole them from up the hill.' In court at Wandsworth on this day, Young stated he did not wish to be remanded but wanted immediate trial and sentence. When he was told he would be sent to Surrey Sessions, Young asked if he could be tried at the Old Bailey. The answer was in the negative but Young seemed happy to get back to prison life – he left the courtroom dancing!

17 JUNE 1886

Thomas Lucas, a ticket-of-leave man (i.e. released early on licence from prison) who kept a stewed-eel shop in Snow's Fields, Bermondsey, was brought up on remand for cutting and unlawfully wounding his daughter and her friend with a butcher's knife. Lucas had only just been released from serving a twelve-year prison sentence for stabbing his wife in 1876! Lucas was committed for trial.

18 JUNE 1895

Joseph Canning (32), a male nurse, was executed at Wandsworth for the murder of his sweetheart, Jane Youell.

19 JUNE 1888

Dennis Harney appeared at Thames Police Court for discharging a revolver at PC John Welley 429H. Welley had been on duty at Stepney railway station on Commercial Road when at 12.35 a.m. he spotted Harney and four other men staggering down the street and singing at the top of their voices. Welley told them to stop or he would have to charge them with disturbing the peace. Harney ran into a shop doorway and continued singing. PC Welley warned him again and Harney, who had been joined by two others, ran off. He then stopped suddenly, raised his arm and a gunshot followed. PC Welley blew his whistle and gave chase. Harney was arrested and brought into custody. The magistrate stated it could not be proven that Harney shot at PC Welley and Harney swore blind the pistol went off in his pocket. Harney was found guilty of 'firing a revolver recklessly in a public thoroughfare' and fined 40s or one month with hard labour.

A teenage mother sketched from life in an East End dosshouse, c. 1888.

20 JUNE Life and Death in the Abyss: Poetry from the Ghetto

This poem from *The Ghetto* in *People of the Abyss* by Jack London sums up much of the atmosphere of the hardest parts of the East End in the late nineteenth century.

Is it well that while we range with Science,
  glorying in the time,
City children soak and blacken soul and
  sense in city slime?
There among the gloomy alleys, progress
  halts on palsied feet.
Crime and hunger cast out maidens by
  the thousand on the street;s

There the master scrimps his haggard seamstress of her daily bread;
There the single sordid attic holds the living and the dead;
There the smouldering fire of fever creeps across the rotted floor,
And the crowded couch of incest, in the warrens of the poor.

21 JUNE 1888

William Pailes (15), Richard Blowe and Isaac Freeman (11) appeared at Thames Police Court charged with being concerned in the theft of four shillings from the till of Joshua Reynolds, confectioner, of 52 Devon Road, Bromley. When the young reprobates entered the shop, Arthur Upton the shop boy, came through to attend on them. Blowe immediately knocked him down, Pailes held his mouth and Freeman grabbed the money. Found guilty, Pailes and Blowe were remanded but Freeman incurred the wrath of the magistrate who ordered him to be 'immediately flogged'.

22 JUNE 1900

Catherine Amelia Irwin (35) was murdered by her estranged husband William James Irwin (61), a cooper. Having been separated from Catherine (his second wife) for a few months, Irwin became jealous when she seemed to be spending increasing amounts of time with another man named Sexton. Irwin's anger also increased when over several occasions he asked her for money and she always said she had none. On 21 June 1900 he had asked her again and received the same response. A row soon developed and William said she had just driven the last nail into her coffin. He accosted her again the following morning while she was walking to work with a colleague, Emily Wright. Catherine pulled away, saying she had to get to work. William then plunged a knife into her breast, piercing her right lung, and she died later that day at the Middlesex Hospital. In court Irwin claimed he acted in a moment of passion and could only be guilty of manslaughter, but the jury thought otherwise and he was found guilty of murder and sentenced to death. The execution was carried out by James Billington at Newgate on 14 August 1900.

23 JUNE 1886

Mary Ann Brown (29) was brought before Lambeth Court on charges of assault and drunkenness. It emerged that a Mr Matthews was passing through St Mary's Square when Brown approached Matthews and asked him to stand treat for a drink. He refused and walked on but Brown was not to be deterred. Seizing hold of him, she said she would not let go until he gave her a shilling. A passing policeman noticed the incident and went to break it up but was met by a tirade of abusive language from Brown. She was found guilty on both counts and sentenced to three weeks with hard labour.

24 JUNE Prisons and Punishments: The Treadmill

The treadmill was introduced to London by the Suffolk engineer and iron founder William Cubitt, and the first in the capital was installed at Brixton Prison in 1821 for the grand sum of £6,913 3s 6d. The principle of the treadmill was simple. It was turned by men climbing steps on the periphery of a cylinder or wheel. Each contained 24 steps set 8in apart, so the circumference of the mill was 16ft. Under the power of the convicts walking up its 'steps' it revolved twice in a minute with a mechanism set to ring a bell on every thirtieth revolution to announce that the spell of work was finished. Every man put to labour at the wheel worked fifteen quarter-hour sessions, climbing up to 19,000ft every day. Some mills had purposes. The one at Brixton was used to grind corn and the one at Holloway pumped water, but most drove nothing. The one at Newgate simply spun great windmill sails on the roof of the gaol. In 1895 there were thirty-nine treadmills and twenty-nine cranks in use in British prisons. Treadmills were finally banned by an Act of Parliament in 1898. (See also 3 December, p. 180.)

25 JUNE Tales from the Abyss: Hospital Scraps

When Jack London visited the Whitechapel Workhouse, he was tasked with joining the infirmary working party; tea was brought to them in the cellar with 'hospital scraps'. He recorded the event in *People of the Abyss*: 'These were heaped high on a huge platter in an indescribable mess – pieces of bread, chunks of grease and fat pork, the burnt skin from the outside of roasted joints, bones, in short, all the leavings from the fingers and mouths of the sick. . . . Into this mess men plunged their hands, digging, pawing, turning over, examining. . . . But the poor devils were hungry, and they ate ravenously of the swill.'

The desperate and homeless in the Salvation Army Shelter at Blackfriars, *c.* 1890. Known as the 'penny sit-up' it was the cheapest paid lodgings in London – pay a penny and sit on a bench in the shelter all night.

·THE THAMES MYSTERY·

THE BODY IN THE BATH – AT THE WANDSWORTH UNION.   OTHER PORTIONS OF THE BODY IN SPIRITS

26 June 1889

The final report on body parts found floating in the Thames and on the shoreline appeared in *The Times*. Throughout late May and June 1889 newspapers detailed body parts being washed up on the shore or picked upon the great river. The body was identified by means of old scars as that of Elizabeth Jackson. The only possible clue to the identity of the murderer was that some of the body parts had been wrapped in clothing bearing the name tape of 'L E Fisher'. Nobody was ever brought to justice for this foul deed.

27 June 1889

The shooting of acrobat and trick cyclist George Gorin, better known as George Letine (36), leader of 'The Wonderful Letines', hit the headlines. Gorin was entering the Canterbury Theatre of Varieties on Westminster Bridge Road when Nathaniel Curragh (53) stepped up beside him and plunged a blade into his abdomen. Before the passers-by could understand what had occurred Gorin was slumping towards the floor, Curragh crossed to the other side of the road, put a pistol in his mouth and pulled the trigger. The bullet lodged in the roof of his mouth and his life was saved at St Thomas's Hospital. It emerged that Curragh's daughter had been a member of the Letines but left about a year previous. She died shortly after and Curragh believed her death was in some way due to her training at the hands of Gorin. Curragh was found 'unsound of mind' and ordered to be detained at Her Majesty's pleasure.

28 June 1892

Charles William Wheeler was charged at Marylebone Court for attempting to stab PC Begg 632M. Begg had entered a house upon hearing cries of 'murder' and discovered a drunk Wheeler chasing his wife about the house with a knife. PC Begg told Mrs Wheeler to go to the police station. She got out but when she had gone Wheeler launched himself at Begg. A mortal struggle ensued in which Begg's tunic was

St Paul's Cathedral, a symbol of hope, soaring about the grimy city, *c*. 1888.

punctured and his chest scratched by a very near miss from the blade. Wheeler was committed for trial – it was noted that over ten warrants had been issued against him for violent behaviour over the years.

29 June 1874

First private execution of a woman at Newgate. Frances 'Fanny' Stewart (43) was executed at Newgate for the murder of her infant grandson. Mrs Stewart was a widow who lived with her daughter and son-in-law and their 12-month-old child in Chelsea. On 27 April Mrs Stewart had a trifling quarrel with her son-in-law, and in the evening she and the child were found to be missing. Fanny Stewart wrote to her son-in-law, stating she would make his heart ache as hers did, threatening suicide for the baby and herself. A second letter to the daughter confessed the murder of the child and begged her to meet and give her over to the police, which was done. The body of the child was recovered from the river off Millwall on 7 May. After sentence was passed she 'accepted her fate with earnestness' and wrote a letter full of penitence to her daughter. Fanny Stewart went to the gallows with 'remarkable courage'. Her struggles after the drop fell 'were momentarily prolonged by some unfortunate twisting of the rope'.

30 June 1891

Alfred Bachert, the chairman of the Whitechapel Murder Vigilance Committee, who described himself as an engraver and reporter of 13 Newnham Street, Whitechapel, was charged at Thames Police Court with disorderly conduct and causing a crowd to assemble on Whitechapel High Street. Constable 325H said he had seen Bachert fighting and was aware he had been ejected from a certain butcher's shop no less than four times that evening. Bachert still refused to leave the shop and was taken into custody. Bachert was found guilty and ordered to pay 5s or five days in default.

JULY

Cleopatra's Needle, photographed here *c.* 1888, was beset by numerous misfortunes and disasters. The 'needle' was fully encased in a vessel named *Cleopatra* and was towed across the oceans from Egypt by the British steamship *Olga*. During a violent storm off the Bay of Biscay the tow ropes had to be cut and six men from the *Olga* were drowned in their attempts to rescue the men of the *Cleopatra*. Thought to have been lost, the *Cleopatra* was sighted again, towed into Ferrol Harbour and eventually towed to England by the paddle tug *Anglia* and was finally erected on the Embankment in 1878. The two bronze sphinxes, cast at the Ecclestone Iron works in Pimlico, were added in 1881. At night this monument, originally created before Christ walked the earth, has an eerie quality and, over the years, has been the scene of more suicides than any other London landmark.

1 JULY 1895

Death down the drain. Work needed to be carried out down one of the drains of the East Ham Sewage Works, and so the manhole cover was removed and Walter Digby went to let one of his workmates, Charles King, know he was about to commence work down the hole. King waited at the top of the hole to make sure Digby descended safely. Digby called up that he felt faint and was returning to the surface. When he was two rungs from the top, he appeared to be overcome and fell back down into the blackness with a sickening squelch as he hit the bottom. King called for help and Mr Frederic Mills, the chief engineer, with Robert Durrant, Arthur Rutter and Frederick Jones came running and descended into the hole one after the other. However, 'all seemed overcome and fell down the hole without saying a word'. A very shaken Charles King went for further assistance. All the bodies were eventually recovered. Only Frederick Jones was brought out alive from that drain, and he died in hospital the following day.

2 JULY Prisons and Punishments: Oakum Picking

This was a common occupation set for prisoners during the nineteenth century. The process could be carried out in solitary confinement cells or with other prisoners (in silence) in workrooms or oakum sheds. It involved the prisoner being given a weighed amount of old ship's rope, often black with tar and deeply engrained with salt and cut into lengths. The rope was separated into its corkscrewed strands, and these would then be un-rolled by sliding them back and forth on the knee with the palm of the hand until the yarns were loosened. The yarns or threads were then separated and cleaned of the salt and tar on them. This 'stuff' was used for caulking the seams in the sides and decks of wooden ships. Men, women and children prisoners all picked oakum. It was very hard on the fingers and rope cuts were common, as were blisters, which proved very painful until the skin on the hands hardened to the work. Prisoners were expected to produce between three and four pounds every two hours. Shifts of oakum picking could last up to twelve hours. At Tothill Fields the boys (all under 17) could earn up to 17s a year for their oakum pickings – literally money for old rope!

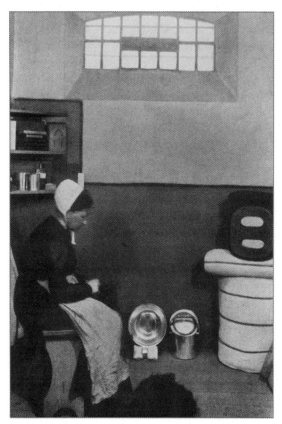

Female inmate picking oakum in her cell at Wormwood Scrubs Prison, *c.* 1895.

3 JULY 1891

William Warren (19), a costermonger, appeared before Lambeth Court having been observed severely beating his horse by Mr Harris the street inspector. Halting the cart, Harris noticed the horse was 'nothing more than a bag of bones'. Found guilty of beating and working an unfit horse Warren was sentenced to one month's hard labour.

4 JULY 1888

Charles Latham (30) was indicted for the wilful murder of Mary Newman. Latham and Newman had been living together for some months; Latham had taken to drinking and begun to get increasingly paranoid about Mary Newman's feelings for another resident, a Mr Salmon, at their Somers Town lodgings. Latham attacked Newman and Salmon but was diagnosed with delirium tremens and taken to the infirmary. Discharged as cured on 7 May, he soon started drinking again. On 19 May he was seized by another drunken fit of rage and set about Newman with a table knife. Her cries soon raised assistance and medical help was soon present, but she died shortly afterwards. Latham was taken into police custody and was observed to be 'behaving in a strange manner and rolling his eyes in a most unnatural way'. He was declared insane and to be 'detained until Her Majesty's Pleasure be known'.

5 JULY 1888

Bryant & May's match girls' strike, 1888. The working conditions for many in late nineteenth-century London were absolutely horrendous, and workers were crammed into sweatshops, cobbling boots, making clothes, rubber, soap and fashioning metalware, etc. One of the most horrible places to work was in a match factory, where much of the labour force were women and children. Many were made sick by the chemicals they were exposed to, which caused loss of breath. One condition, which was known as 'Phossy Jaw', was particularly nasty. The ingested phosphorous caused gums to rot and teeth to fall out, and eventually it ate into and destroyed live bone. The homeward paths of the workers could always be traced by the luminous vomit which gathered in the gutters along the way. In 1888 social reformer Annie Besant led the girls to down tools on this day and they successfully went on strike for better working conditions and wages.

6 JULY 1889

Inspector Frederick Abberline arrived at 19 Cleveland Street in the West End to arrest Charles Hammond. The warrant Abberline carried pulled no punches, spelling out the charges of 'unlawfully, wickedly, and corruptly conspire, combine, confederate and agree to . . . procure teenage prostitutes to commit the abominable crime of buggery'. Hammond had fled but his accomplice Henry Newlove (18) was soon traced and apprehended. Closure of a homosexual brothel and the prosecution of its keepers was hardly headline news, but this case was different. Soon the names of eminent and titled gentlemen were being given and corroborated by the brothel's operatives. Rumours of the scandal began to circulate but were stamped on with a heavy boot from the highest levels when Eddy, Duke of Clarence, son of Edward Prince of Wales (later Edward VII) (see also 14 January, p. 17) and imminent heir to the throne of England became implicated in what became known as the 'Cleveland Street Scandal'.

7 July 1888

Hard eggs! The case was reported of Henry Shepherd (53), a labourer 'of no home', who had no money and being starving hungry stole four eggs (formally valued in court at 6*d*) from a henhouse at Holloway Farm, South End, Lewisham. Found guilty, Shepherd was sentenced to fourteen days with hard labour.

8 July 1888

In the streets of the East End many groups of children played on or beside the road. Despite the traffic being horse-drawn and nothing like as busy as it is today, sometimes there were accidents. On this day little David Cavalier (1 year and 10 months old) was playing in front of his parents' lodgings at Warner Place, off Hackney Road. His mother noticed the fish merchant's cart approaching with the driver standing and whipping the horses. She rushed out to pull the child to safety, but little David thought he was going to be admonished and ran into the road. The mother and child were hit by the cart and killed. The driver, Tarplett, who was found to have been drinking 'but was not drunk', stood trial and was found not guilty of manslaughter.

9 July Prisons and Punishments: Whitecross Street Prison

This was the last of the old city compters or debtors' gaols (used for debtors and minor offenders). Construction had begun in 1813 and its first inmates, who took up their cells in 1815, were the last debtors from Newgate Prison. For most of the nineteenth century severe debt carried a prison sentence. The only way for people to get out was to pay their debts, but it was no easy matter to earn money in prison. Debtors would sit at their window or hole and beg passers-by for money; begging letters frequently appeared in newpapers; and families made destitute by the main breadwinner frequently ended up having to live with them in the gaol! Charles Dickens spoke with authority about debtors' prisons in *Little Dorrit*, his father having been imprisoned for three months for debt in Marshalsea Prison in 1824. The purpose of Whitecross Street Prison was ultimately negated by the 1869 Debtor's Act and the last twenty-seven prisoners were removed to Holloway in July 1870. The old prison was demolished in 1877 to make a way for a railway goods yard. The site is now covered by the Barbican development.

10 JULY 1872

A double mystery. The dead body of Mrs Sarah Squires, who kept the paper shop at 46 Hyde Road, Hoxton, was discovered behind the counter by a young lad named Eyre. Police were summoned and when the premises were searched, the body of her daughter, Christiana, was discovered at the top of the kitchen stairs. Both had been bludgeoned to death. The motive was assumed to be robbery, because boxes and drawers had been forced open. Despite extensive enquiries their murderer was never discovered. This tale has a peculiar twist: fifteen years later, on Tuesday 15 August 1888, Thomas Wright (36), a chair maker of Roden Street, Holloway, casually handed himself over to Inspector Alfred Woodley of Y Division. Wright had already confessed to a cabman. After asking directions to the police station where he would give himself up, Wright said to the cabby, 'They have been looking out for me for fifteen years. . . . Do you recollect the Hoxton murder? Mrs Squires and her daughter about fifteen years ago. I did it with a crowbar.' Scotland Yard was called in and Wright was brought before the magistrate at Worship Street where evidence was presented by Detective Inspector Peel of G Division. The facts were clear: 'The prisoner was at work at the time of the murder and could not have done it.' The magistrate was furious with Wright for wasting police time and remarked he 'regretted he had not the power to send the prisoner to gaol'. Wright was discharged. The murder has never been solved, and nor has any reason appeared as to why Wright should have confessed to a murder committed fifteen years previously.

11 JULY 1871

Edward Welsh (29), a bellhanger, and William Williams (27), a packing-crate maker, appeared before Thames Police Court charged with mugging Henry Flint on the Strand. Mr Flint was walking home shortly after 11 p.m. on 26 June when Welsh rushed out of the shadows of George Court, struck a blow to his cheek, and grabbed and snapped away Flint's watch chain complete with the old guinea piece and two rings attached to it. Flint attempted to give chase but was blocked by Williams. A constable was soon on the scene and Williams was taken into custody and Welsh traced and arrested from a description given by Flint. Williams received twelve months' hard labour. Welsh had previous convictions of six and three years; he was thus sentenced to ten years' penal servitude.

12 JULY 1888

An evening inquest was held at the Board Room, Mount Street, Grosvenor Square, into the death of Sir John Hardy (79) of Burton upon Trent, who died at his London residence in South Street, Park Lane, of injuries sustained after being knocked down by a brougham carriage belonging to Miss Hope of Cumberland Place. Sir John had gone to post a letter in the pillar box near the corner of South Audley Street, and while crossing the road in the direction of Berkeley Square he was knocked down by the horse or shafts of the brougham and broke his thigh. Witnesses stated that the coachman had shouted out to Sir John two or three times as he rounded the corner, but there was too much traffic about to avoid the accident. Dr Francis Laking attended Sir John at his home but after four days poor Sir John lost his battle for life. The jury recorded 'accidental death' and a recommendation was made that in future a policeman should be stationed at the corner where the accident happened.

13 JULY 1885

Henry Alt, a German national, was executed at Newgate for the murder of Charles Howard. The case was simple and horrible. Alt had 'paid his address' to a widow who changed her mind in favour of marrying Charles Howard. She chose a time when Howard was present to tell Alt. Alt went mad with jealousy and attacked Howard with a dagger, inflicting wounds he soon died from. He then set about the woman who had rejected him, and finally himself. Alt was not successful in killing the woman or himself. The trial was straightforward and a death sentence was passed on Alt. On the days leading up to his execution Alt paid great attention to the ministrations of the prison chaplain and 'expressed himself ready to die'. Executioner Berry guided Alt's last steps on to the gallows, pinioned him and placed the cap over his head. As Berry adjusted the noose Alt spoke out that he believed he was in his situation 'all through a deceitful woman and that he had evidence –' His statement was silenced by the fall of the gallows trapdoors.

14 JULY 1882

A hero twice over! PC Jenkins 233E was on duty on Waterloo Bridge when at 2 a.m. he saw a man named Chapman jump from the bridge into the river. Taking off his coat, Jenkins dived into the river and, with the aid of the Thames Police, managed to rescue the man. PC Jenkins was awarded the Stanhope Gold Medal and Royal Humane Society Silver Medal for his bravery. On 3 June PC Jenkins was on duty with PC Amber on the Victoria Embankment when they saw a woman jump over the parapet into the river. The PCs ran down to the pier and Jenkins jumped in, caught hold of the woman and endeavoured to keep her afloat. She struggled violently and after three or four minutes Jenkins could hold her no more and she drowned. Jenkins had to be assisted from the water and was taken to Charing Cross Hospital where he made a full recovery.

15 JULY 1890

Aaron Kosminski was discharged from Mile End Workhouse to his brother's care. Kosminski was known to the police and was named by Macnaghten in his list of suspects (see 23 February, p. 38): 'This man became insane owing to many years' indulgence in solitary vices. He had a great hatred of women, specially of the prostitute class, & had strong homicidal tendencies.' Kosminski had a history of mental illness, and his family had tried hard to have him certified. On the first attempt in 1890 he had been held for three days before being released to his brother-in-law. On 4 February

Westminster Bridge and St Thomas's Hospital viewed from the Victoria Embankment side of the river, *c.* 1888. Experienced policemen always kept a weather eye out on the bridges of London which had steps descending beside the waters' edge. They knew many potential suicides would attempt to ease themselves into the water at these points because they stood more of a chance of changing their mind than after choosing to dive from a bridge parapet.

1891 he was readmitted and, after an examination by Dr Edmund King, committed on 7 February to Colney Hatch Asylum. He was transferred to Leavesden Asylum near Watford in 1894, where he remained until his death in 1919 (see also 6 December, p. 182)

16 JULY 1888

Agnes Norman (15), a domestic servant, was indicted for the murder of Jessie Jane Beer. The were also three other charges of murder against her and an indictment of attempt to murder. The main case against Norman was from Mr Beer who had left his three perfectly healthy children in her care when he and his wife went out for the afternoon and evening on 7 April (Good Friday). When they returned shortly before midnight, they found Norman asleep in a chair – all the children were in bed. When one of the children was heard to start crying Beer went upstairs. Sharing the room was the Beers' 15-month-old daughter, Jessie. Disturbed that the baby didn't even stir when the child started crying, Mr Beer soon found to his horror that the little mite was dead. Joseph Lees, a surgeon on the Walworth Road, was called and pronounced the baby's death was due to suffocation. In courtroom cross-examination the surgeon had to admit the appearance of the baby's death was 'not inconsistent with death being accidental'. Because the jury could not exclude other causes of death, it was directed accordingly and the murder charges were quashed. She then stood trial for the attempted murder of one of her previous employers' children, and evidence was given about a 10-year-old boy named Charles Parfitt who had woken from his slumbers to find Norman's hand across his nose and mouth. The boy's aunt (with whom he lived) heard his stifled cry and rushed upstairs to see Norman getting off young Charles's bed. Norman was found guilty, and before sentence was passed the judge stated that 'there was no moral doubt that she was morally responsible' for the deaths she stood trial for earlier. In passing sentence, the judge said the purpose of his punishment was 'to restrain her for some years from the fatal fascination which seemed to have possessed her'. Norman was sent down for fifteen years' penal servitude.

17 July

Fears of a return of the Ripper. The body of Alice McKenzie, who was known on the streets as 'Claypipe Alice', was discovered by PC Walter Andrews 272H about 12.50 a.m. between two carts in the Whitechapel High Street end of Castle Alley. Andrews used his whistle and was soon joined by Sergeant Badham. Blood was still flowing from a slash across her throat, and her abdomen had received cuts from a knife. Dr Phillips was summoned to the crime scene and the body of 'Claypipe Alice' was removed to the Whitechapel Mortuary. The doctors disagreed as to the hand of the perpetrator. Dr Phillips considered the wounds not so severe or direct as those inflicted by the Ripper, whereas Dr Bond was of the opinion 'the murder was performed by the same person who committed the former series of Whitechapel murders'. The day after the murder William Wallace Brodie walked into Leman Street police station and gave himself up, claiming to be 'Jack the Ripper'. His outlandish claims and strange mannerisms led to an assessment of his mental state. Brodie was remanded for the murder of McKenzie but was discharged on account of his mental problems. Brodie was later rearrested for fraud.

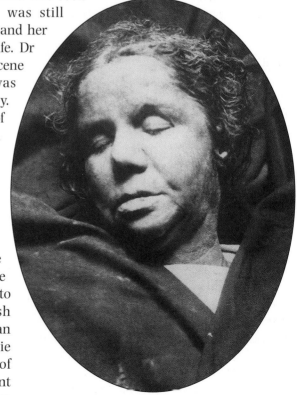

Mortuary photograph of Alice McKenzie.
(Stewart P. Evans)

18 July 1871

The case was reported of Charles (41) and Sarah de Baddeley (37) of 4 Exeter Villas, Kensington, who appeared at the Central Criminal Court. They had placed an advertisement in a spiritualist journal inviting people to consult at the house. The police sent a woman named Hansard with a fictitious enquiry on behalf of a pregnant friend to visit 'Madame de Baddeley' to elicit her mode of procedure. Madame gave Hansard a quantity of ergot of rye to procure abortion. The sum of 6s was paid in total to Madame de Baddeley. Mr and Mrs de Baddeley insisted they had committed no crime and criticised the police for laying a trap. The jury found both guilty and they were sentenced to twelve months' hard labour.

19 July 1871

Catherine Hatch, 'a middle-aged governess' at the Fan Street infant school, Bow Common, appeared before Thames Police Court charged with 'unmercifully flogging Richard Godard', a boy of only 4 years old. The child had been brought before Mr Paget the magistrate who said he had 'never seen a child in such a shocking condition'. The boy's sister stated he had been stripped and flogged with a leather strap because 'he had been very naughty and bit teacher's hand'. The court found the teacher guilty and as a warning to those teachers 'who abused the power invested in them' Miss Hatch was sent down for fourteen days with hard labour!

20 July 1898

A report was published of the inquest into the deaths of Walter Peart and Henry Dean of Kentish town, respectively driver and stoker of the 4.15 p.m. Great Western express train from Windsor to Paddington. On the stretch of line between Ealing and Acton, the steam engine's connecting rod broke and the fire box and boiler were so damaged that the cab was instantly filled with fire and steam. Despite being horribly burnt, both driver and firemen fought in this hell to bring the train to a standstill. Both were removed to St Mary's Hospital, Paddington, where they both died of their injuries. Both were married men, and Peart left five children. A subscription was set up in aid of their families.

21 July 1891

Franz Joseph Münch (31), a native of Coblenz employed as a journeyman baker, was executed at Wandsworth for the murder of James Hickey at Bermondsey. On the morning of the execution Münch rose at 6.30a.m. and accompanied Father Galerau, the Roman Catholic priest to the prison chapel where the sacrament was administered. At five minutes to nine Captain Helby, the prison governor and Mr F. Kynaston Metcalfe, the under sheriff, proceeded to the condemned cell with James Berry the public executioner. As Münch was pinioned he thanked the prison officials for their kindness and walked purposefully to the scaffold. All was over by the final chimes of the clock and the body was left to hang for the typical hour after the drop. Death appeared to be instantaneous, but at the inquest before Mr A. Braxton Hicks (of contractions fame), Dr Richard F. Quinton stated that death was by strangulation, there being no fracture or dislocation of the neck. However, the law had still been carried out – death was by hanging – broken neck or not.

22 JULY People of the Streets: The Salvation Army Workers

The Salvation Army was established by William Booth (1829–1912) in a large tent erected on a Quaker burial ground at the Mile End Waste on Sunday 2 July 1865. Booth's message was clear: he rejected the Victorian idea of the 'deserving poor' and believed passionately that if a man was poor he was deserving. Booth's work was truly tireless, and despite initial suspicion and even attacks on their parades and meetings, Booth persevered and began to see his army of Christian volunteer workers gradually grow. Many of these workers were women. The workers visited slums and common lodging houses and attempted to reach as many as they could in the East End to try to guide them on to the straight and narrow of Christian values and abstinence. This was not without its dangers and costs to the 'Sally Army Slum Saviours' who helped nurse and attend those in need and poverty in the East End. They were be exposed to the same germs and diseases as those they cared for, and many of these 'Saviours' had their lives prematurely curtailed because of their noble work among the poverty-stricken. The feeding of the destitute and the poor remained paramount for the Salvation Army. They established soup kitchens in which large bowls of good soup were served with slabs of bread for a penny to those who could afford to pay, and free to those who were penniless. Basic shelter was also provided for those who had none. On 18 February 1888 a former warehouse on the West India Docks was opened by Booth for the purpose of lodging and feeding the destitute at 3d a night. Prayers and an invitation to be 'saved' were part of the deal; so was good food and even clean sheets on every one of the 150 beds. Booth was soon to open further hostels for mothers and unwanted children in the East End. The work and hostels of the Salvation Army eventually spread all over the world, and their work still goes on today.

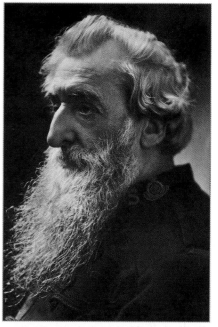

General William Booth, founder of the Salvation Army.

One of the 'Sally Army Slum Saviours', c. 1888.

23 JULY Life and Death in the Abyss: Dr Barnardo

One of the greatest hopes for young people born and cast out into the abyss of the East End was the great philanthropist Dr Thomas John Barnardo (1845–1905). Deeply moved by the life of destitute children in the East End, Dr Barnardo opened his first home for destitute boys at 18 Stepney Causeway in 1870. This home had just twenty-five places, and the agony of deciding who were to be the twenty-five boys lucky enough to be admitted haunted Barnardo for the rest of his life. The twenty-sixth boy was an 11-year-old lad named John Somers, whose bright ginger hair gave him the nickname of 'Carrots'. He barely existed on the occasional work he had as a bootblack and paper-seller. He was not selected because it was found he still had a living parent, a mother, whereas the other boys had nobody. Some days later a Billingsgate porter was moving a barrel when he disturbed two waifs; one ran off, the other remained motionless. It was 'Carrots', and he was dead through hunger and exposure. Barnardo saw this as a salutary lesson and erected a sign above the door of No. 18 which was never to be removed: 'NO DESTITUTE CHILD EVER REFUSED ADMISSION', with the addendum underneath of 'Open all night'. By 1905, when he died, Barnardo's children's homes occupied 102 buildings in London and beyond and over 59,384 children had been saved through their care. The great work of Barnardo's is still going strong today.

24 JULY 1893

Charles Suett (47), a hawker, appeared at Thames Police Court charged with housebreaking. He had been arrested on the Whitechapel Road after a quantity of stolen plate was found hidden under straw and cucumbers on the back of his pony cart. He was only brought in after a fierce struggle with detectives. Several previous convictions (two of ten-year stretches) counted heavily against Suett and he was sentenced to another ten years.

Dr Thomas Barnardo.

25 JULY 1893

The only Metropolitan police officer to be hanged. PC George Samuel Cooke met Maud Merton (a.k.a. Smith, Crowcher or Locksley), a prostitute, about 1891. Cooke desperately tried to reform her but she continued to walk the streets. After quarrels and rent arrear issues with their landlady, Cooke threatened to leave Merton. She turned nasty and made a chain of allegations to Cooke's superior officer. His senior did not believe the stories, but because Cooke was being indiscreet with 'an unfortunate', he was disciplined and transferred. He formed a new attachment with a ladies' maid and their engagement was soon announced. Maud heard of this and could not bear it. She traced Cooke to his beat patrolling the common near Wormwood Scrubs. Their argument resulted in Cooke seeing red. He drew his truncheon, felled Maud with it, smashing her skull, and stamped on her neck. Her body was discovered by a shepherd the following day. Cooke soon confessed to the crime. At his trial a number of the jurors wished to bring a verdict of manslaughter but Justice Hawkins ended up putting on the black cap and Cooke was hanged on 25 July.

26 JULY 1888

A true recidivist. Walter Johnson (62) began his five years of penal servitude for possession of four counterfeit shilling pieces. Johnson had been arrested on Lancaster Road, Borough. He was brought in after a violent struggle and the four coins were found. It was soon found that Johnson had spent more time in prison than out. In recent times he had had separate sentences of two, eight and ten years – all for passing bad money!

27 JULY 1887

A presentation was made to Police Sergeant Barker by Metropolitan Police Commissioner Sir Charles Warren at Holborn Town Hall. In March the brave sergeant had attempted to capture two burglars single-handedly. When he got his hands on one, the other brutally set about him with an iron bar. He was left in an unconscious state on the railway and a passing train cut off his right foot. The brave policeman was well looked after for his bravery: he could no longer work but he was granted a pension of £78 a year for life. At the presentation Barker was given a testimonial on vellum, a marble timepiece and the £622 raised from charitable contributions.

28 JULY 1873

The Lincoln Court tragedy. Fire broke out at 8 Lincoln Court, off Great Wild Street. Ellen Donovan (37), a neighbour at No. 10, knew children to be at No. 8 and had not seen them evacuate the building. Rushing inside, she ran upstairs amid a house full of flame and smoke. The tragedy was that this selfless act was unnccccssary because the children were all out of the building. Ellen's escape route was blocked as the stairs erupted into a mass of flames and her remains were only recovered after the fire had been extinguished.

The execution of Kate Webster.

29 JULY 1879

Kate Webster was executed at Wandsworth. Webster was an Irish con woman who took up a position as cook and general servant to widow Mrs Julia Martha Thomas, at her residence of 2 Mayfield Park Villas, Park Road, Richmond, in January 1879. Thomas was known for her reputation as a tartar towards her servants and could never keep staff long. Although Webster was initially glad of honest work, she felt the workload was greatly increased as time went on, and her work was criticised by the mistress. Finally, in the February, she had had enough and gave notice to Webster, thus potentially rendering her and her illegitimate son destitute.

The atmosphere built day by day as she worked her notice until the Sunday before she was set to leave, when Webster and Thomas had a huge argument. Mrs Thomas went to her religious meeting where she was described as 'excited and flushed'. From the early hours of the following morning, washing and brushing were heard coming from the villa, a full complement of washing was hung out, and all seemed normal. However, when Webster started appearing in Mrs Thomas's clothes and selling them, stern questions about where she was began to be asked. Webster fled to Killanne, Ireland, but was soon traced, brought to trial and found guilty of murder. The villa abounded with clues. Poor Mrs Thomas had been cut up and boiled and burnt on the kitchen and copper grates. The gentlefolk of London no doubt had a little shiver when reading this case, but I wonder how those who had bought the gallipots of meat-dripping hawked by Webster felt when they heard how she had dealt with her boss?

30 JULY 1888

Patrick Lynch (38), a tailor of Noel Street, Soho, and his wife were charged with neglecting to provide proper nourishment and food for their four children (Charlotte, 4; Michael, 2; and twin boys Frank and Henry, 10 months). Prosecuted by the guardians of St James's Westminster, it was stated that the children had been found in an emaciated state at the Noel Street lodgings. The parents earned as much as £10 a week but due to 'shocking intemperance' little or nothing was spent on the children. Found guilty, both parents were sentenced to three months with hard labour.

31 JULY 1893

John O'Brien (35) of 5 Duke Street, Aldgate, was brought before the Guildhall Court for assaulting his wife. During a day of arguments he had thrown a heavy box at her and later kicked her in the head while she lay in bed. She had had to be hospitalised. Corroborative evidence was given and O'Brien was sentenced to six months with hard labour.

AUGUST

✝

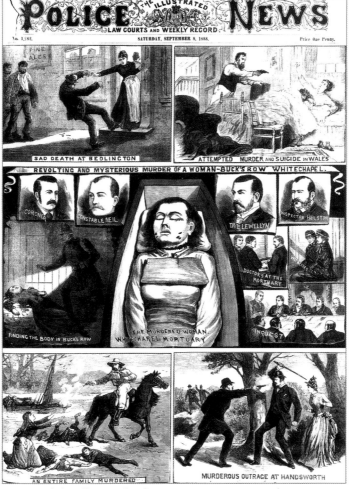

Cover of the *Illustrated Police News*. Centre page is the story in pictures of the horrible murder of Polly Nichols, discovered on Buck's Row, Whitechapel, 31 August 1888. This crime is thought by many to be the first in a short but hideous series of killings in the East End of London by an unknown person who was soon dubbed Jack the Ripper. *(Stewart P. Evans)*

1 August 1870

Walter Millar (31) was executed at the Old Bailey for the murder of the Revd Elias Huelin (84) and his housekeeper, Mrs Ann Boss, at their residence in Chelsea. The crime was described by *The Times* as a 'horrible and revolting atrocity'. Millar, a plasterer by trade, had attempted a deception whereby he planned to remove goods and valuables from the house of the reverend by pretending to be his nephew. When it went wrong, he killed the reverend and his housekeeper – they were found battered to death with ropes around their necks. Millar admitted his guilt and never showed any contrition for his crimes. As the day of execution approached, he was kept under suicide watch. As the hour of execution approached Millar did manage to elude the vigilance of his warder and charged head first at the wall. He stunned himself and had to lie on a mattress on the floor. Refusing or unable to rise when the executioner entered the cell, he was pinioned in that prostrate position and carried to the gallows in a chair by nine warders in a procession led by the prison chaplain. Still sat in the chair he was placed on the gallows trap, the rope was adjusted around his neck and he was sent to his doom with chair and all.

2 August Criminal Types: Female Pickpockets

Rather like the garotter (see 22 February, p. 37), the female pickpocket was often more successful than the male in late Victorian Britain. Gentlemen, drunk or not, would always try to maintain an air of upright pride and middle-class values if approached by a pretty young lady. Few men would push such a young lady off instantly if she greeted him 'mistakenly' as her uncle by placing her arms around him. Her error would no doubt be corrected in a mannered way, but as the gent proceeded to stride off he could well find his wallet and watch chain were missing. Less beautiful older women could show concern for a drunken gentleman, assisting him into a cab, but when he came to pay he might well have found he had been robbed. Cabbies were often in on the act and took a share of the scam. The most base of all female pickpockets robbed those who fell down blind drunk. One girl kept watch while the other 'skinned the stiff'.

3 August 1888

An explosion occurred at the works of Mr H.J. Cadwell, toy firework maker, South Fields, Merton Road, Wandsworth. Luckily most of the factory hands (who were predominantly female) were at dinner. The two fatalities were women who were standing in the doorway of one of the sheds. Their deaths were made all the more tragic when it was realised that the girls were sisters – Lizzie and Eliza Thornton, aged 21 and 19 respectively. Another girl, Lucy Harwood, was badly injured and died a few days later in the Wandsworth and Clapham Union infirmary after her arm had been amputated. When the three buildings affected by the blast were examined, there was hardly a portion of each structure left that was more than a foot in length.

Types of female pickpocket, *c*. 1890.

Explosion at Cadwell's Toy Factory, Wandsworth, 3 August 1888.

4 AUGUST Prisons and Punishments: Brixton Prison

Opened in 1820, this is thus the oldest of London's prisons still receiving prisoners today. Constructed for 175 prisoners to be accommodated in the 'separate system' (see 30 April), it soon crammed 400 into its poorly ventilated and unsanitary cells. In a single year 4,043 prisoners passed through Brixton with 1,085 recorded instances of sickness, including 249 of fever. By 1845 Brixton Prison had become impractical and was proposed to be sold on to the government as a lunatic asylum. After bureaucratic machinations, the Surrey justices sold the buildings to the property developer Sir William Tite, the architect of Norwood Cemetery. By 1853 central government showed interest enough to want to buy back the prison, which they did, giving Sir William a handsome return on his investment. Once in the hands of the prison commissioners, it was expanded and became the first all-women prison. After being a military prison between 1882 and 1897, it was returned to the prison commissioners, who turned it into a remand and short-term sentence prison.

Brixton Prison, *c. 1875*.

5 AUGUST 1889

Henry Ellis (37) appeared on remand at Thames Police Court for shooting a revolver at his estranged wife. Constable Andrews was called to the scene and saw the damaged window and bullet hole in the wall for himself. When Andrews attempted to arrest Ellis, he put up such a fight that Andrews's hand was bitten through in no less than eight places. With the aid of his sister and father, Ellis escaped. (For their trouble his family accomplices got one month's hard labour each). Ellis was eventually brought in. He had already served twenty years for previous misdemeanours and was given another seven years for his rash act.

6 AUGUST 1891

Orlando Bennett (13), Albert Neighbour (14), John Cove (11), William Bennett (12), John Nash (9) and James Cope (9), all of whom lived on Hampden Road, Holloway, were charged with committing shop robberies. All but Albert Neighbour were found guilty. Cope had been in custody four times previously, Nash had been bound over, Cove was 'a troublesome boy' and Bennett had been birched. Cove and Nash, the thieves, were sent to industrial school while one of the accomplices was given twelve strokes of the birch rod and the other two six each.

Mortuary photograph of Martha Tabram.
(Stewart P. Evans)

7 August 1888

Martha Tabram (a.k.a. Emma Turner) (39), a prostitute, was found murdered at about 4.45 a.m. on the first-floor landing of George Yard Buildings, Whitechapel. She had received multiple stab wounds to her chest and abdomen. The post-mortem carried out at the Workhouse Infirmary mortuary on Old Montague Street by Dr Timothy Robert Killeen estimated the time of death as about 2.30 a.m. and suggested that possibly more than one type of instrument had been used. Most of the wounds could have been caused by a knife, but the wound that went straight through the chest bone was inflicted 'by some kind of dagger'. The final statement of the doctor was truly chilling: all of the wounds on Martha Tabram 'were caused during life'. Her friend Mary Ann Connelly, another prostitute, known as 'Pearly Poll', was one of the last people to see her alive. She stated that they had been with Guardsmen, a private and a corporal, for just over an hour when they had divided up, Martha with the private, to go and earn their doss money. Martha was never seen alive again. Poll went under police escort to see the Guards parade at the Tower but she failed to pick anyone out. Wellington Barracks was recorded as rendering every assistance to the police, but Martha's killer was never identified or brought to justice. (See also 31 August, p. 128.)

8 August 1894

The police of K Division, acting under instructions received from Scotland Yard, announced that due to increasing numbers and the growing animosity between the Socialist and Anarchist movements, whose weekend meetings were nearly leading to serious breaches of the peace, the open-air Anarchist meetings at Beckton and Canning Town were to be suppressed. *The Times* commented, 'It is probable that the question of the right of free speech will be tested.'

9 August 1889

George Woodley and William Linsky were charged at Thames Police Court with keeping the Tower Hamlets Club at 65A Whitechapel High Street for the purposes of betting. Forty other men of the neighbourhood were charged with gambling there. Mr Lushington viewed the case 'as a serious one' and fined Woodley £100 plus two shillings costs or three months' prison in default; Linsky was fined £20 or one month's hard labour.

10 AUGUST Criminal Types: The 'Smasher' or 'Coiner'

In the garret rooms of shabby little houses in the poorer areas of London, the 'coiner' plied this criminal trade. Over his coke fire hung a melting pot, an iron ladle before it, and there was an electric battery on the mantel-shelf. On his sturdy table, beside a shapeless mass of bright metal were some oddly formed slabs of plaster of Paris. These were his 'casts' from which he poured the molten metal to make his coins. Wearing a worn leather apron, the 'smasher' was the more senior criminal. Too old to work the streets, or skilled jeweller turned bad, he now used the skill in his hands to file and 'finish' the 'silver' crowns, half-crowns and florins he actually cast in base metal and plated in silver by means of an electroplating process. Once they were ready to enter circulation, the 'coiner' then passed his forged coins to his 'snide pitchers' (see 28 August, p. 128) who either bought the coins at half face value or shared the profits with the 'smasher' after passing the coins as genuine.

11 AUGUST 1881

Aris Alphonso (a native of Madrid) was brought before the Guildhall Court charged with attacking James Isaac Walter, a letter carrier, at his premises on Leadenhall Street. Walter was stabbed in the head and other parts of the body – the weapon was a Spanish double-edged dagger about 10-in long. His case was referred to the Central Criminal Court.

12 AUGUST Prisons and Punishments: Reformatory Schools

Under the Youthful Offenders Act (1854) offenders under 16 could be sent to Reformatory Schools for between two and five years, after fourteen days in prison. The Reformatory Schools were administered by voluntary bodies with aid from state grants. Punishment was an essential part of the strict regime, which included freezing-cold baths, military-style drills and hard physical labour. In 1866 the Industrial School Act created establishments for orphans, children of convicted criminals and refractory children, who would be subject to a strictly instructed basic education and training in industrial and agricultural processes. By the 1870s there were fifty industrial schools for 2,500 needy children and sixty-five Reformatory Schools detaining about 5,000 young offenders. Despite these best efforts juveniles were still being sent to prison well into the 1890s. The Borstal system of reformatory prisons for young offenders guilty of serious or repeat offences was introduced in 1900.

13 AUGUST 1883

The inquest took place into the murder of three toddlers by their father, William Gouldstone (26), blacksmith, of Walthamstow. Gouldstone had complained for some time over his financial difficulties in supporting his family of five children. It was stated that Gouldstone was known to abstain from drink but had often seemed morose and suicidal. He took his three toddlers and 'drowned them like kittens' in a cistern containing just 14in of water. He then stormed into the bedroom where his wife was suckling the twins and swung at her breasts with a hammer. All hell broke loose and the alarm was raised. Taken into custody Gouldstone stated, 'I thought it was getting too hot to have five kids in about three-and-a-half years and thought I would put a stop to it,' adding he was 'ready for the rope'. Gouldstone, whose state of mind was not clearly diagnosed, did not hang for his crimes but was detained 'at Her Majesty's pleasure'.

14 August 1894

Paul Köezula (24) was executed at Newgate. Originally brought to trial with his wife Susannah and accomplice George Schmerfeld, they stood accused of the murder of Mrs Matilda Rasch in her apartments above her husband's continental café and hotel at 167 Shaftesbury Avenue. Mrs Rasch was found strangled by her husband after he returned from a walk with friends. Their two servants, Mr and Mrs Köezula, were missing, as was one of his waiters, George Schmerfeld. An acquaintance of Köezula later testified that as he passed him as he was leaving the hotel that fateful night, Köezula threw the comment at him, 'You'll be surprised tomorrow.' Inspector Reid was soon on the scene and Schmerfeld was rapidly traced to his lodgings, where he was discovered covered in blood, having attempted to take his own life. Good detective work led to the Köezulas at a house on Hackney Road. Stolen goods and money were found on the premises. Although all three were tried, Köezula swore his wife knew nothing of the crime and evidence was presented to such an extent she was acquitted. Both Schmerfeld and Paul Köezula were found guilty and sentenced to death, but Schmerfeld's punishment was commuted to penal servitude. As executioner Billington made his final adjustments, the chaplain asked if Köezula had anything to say. He replied, 'I am innocent.' The execution continued and noisy demonstrations of hostility toward the convict were made by the large crowd assembled outside the prison as the black flag was hoisted.

15 August 1899

Amy Hopkins appeared before West London Police Court for permitting her house at 86 Finborough Road, Kensington, to be used as a brothel. Her husband John, a supervisor at the Earl's Court Exhibition, also appeared on charges of living off immoral earnings. Inspector Seabright of F Division, in describing the character of the house, stated, 'On a recent occasion I saw one of the South African natives enter the house with a woman . . .' After a stream of convincing incidents were related, the couple were found guilty and sentenced to six weeks' imprisonment or £15 fine for Amy and three months' hard labour for John. Three young children, all girls, were rescued from the house; they were ordered by the magistrate to be taken to the workhouse with a view of sending them to industrial schools.

16 AUGUST 1892

The double execution of John George Wenzel and James Taylor took place at Newgate. Wenzel, a young German, had shot Detective Sergeant Joyce when he attempted to arrest him on a charge of larceny. James Taylor, an army pensioner who had served in the Crimea and left with a meritorious army record, beat his wife to death in a drunken rage with a mangle roller. Despite pleas for commutation of his sentence on the grounds of extreme provocation and his good military service, both men kept their appointment with executioner Billington.

17 AUGUST 1888

Walter Scott Hamilton (51), a bookbinder by trade, was admitted on remand to Holloway Prison from Marlborough Street Police Court charged with fraudulently obtaining about £100. All seemed well until the following morning, when Assistant Warder William Brooks went to Hamilton's cell. To his horror he found Hamilton had got on his stool, tied his handkerchief around his neck and to the gas pipe and hung himself. The deceased was cut down and found to have been dead several hours. Mr G.P. Gilbert the prison surgeon gave corroborative evidence at the inquest and the jury returned a verdict of 'suicide while temporarily insane'.

18 AUGUST 1888

Elizabeth Bartlett (56) of 248 Manchester Road, Poplar, was murdered in a fit of rage by her husband, Levi Richard Bartlett. The row had worried the neighbours to the extent that they sent for a constable. Known locally as 'Mad Dick', Bartlett was a habitual drunkard and extremely violent towards his wife and anyone who dared to cross him (or just get in his way). It was later stated that, when drunk, Bartlett had often threatened to cut his wife's head off and throw it in the street. Four constables were sent and discovered Bartlett had cut her throat with his razor and bludgeoned her head. Nothing could be done for her. Bartlett lay beside her on the same bed, having cut his own throat – he was not dead but unconscious. His throat was bound up and he was removed to Poplar hospital – it took four constables and a doctor's assistant to hold him down while the doctor stitched the wound to his neck. Tried at the Central Criminal Court, Bartlett was found guilty and executed by James Berry at Newgate on 13 November 1888.

19 AUGUST Criminal Types: 'The Swell Mobsman'

This character, often of smart appearance, affected some sham foreign title and/or decoration in order to victimise boarding-house keepers in Hampstead or Bloomsbury by passing bogus cheques. A similar looking felon was occasionally to be found at the great railway stations of London. Stepping out from a first-class carriage, he would hail the nearest porter with an authoritative air and get him to hail a hansom cab, declaring he was in a pressing hurry to get to an appointment or to catch a connection at another station. In the press of alighting passengers, he would point out 'his' luggage to the porter, stating it had his printed luggage labels on them. They were loaded on the carriage and he was off, having slapped his labels on someone else's luggage while the porter was hailing his cab!

20 AUGUST 1888

George Hammond (30) was found guilty at Thames Police Court for assaulting Janet Jane Briggs (7) and her mother with a poker. Hammond had lodged with the Briggs family on Narrow Street, Ratcliff, and had come in drunk and threatened to kill them. He then set about those he could find with the poker. Poor little Janet appeared in court with her head still bandaged from the attack. Hammond was found guilty and sentenced to one month with hard labour.

A female inmate of Wandsworth Prison, veiled to comply with the 'silent and separate' system. To enable identification the prisoner wore her identity tag from her waist.

21 AUGUST Prisons and Punishments: Wandsworth

The Surrey House of Correction at Wandsworth was built in 1851 and opened as a prison to accommodate 1,000 prisoners in the 'separate system' on a 26-acre site on the west side of Wandsworth Common. The prison incarcerated those serving short sentences. Few were employed in skilled work, and some convicts were employed in Wandsworth's version of the soul-destroying treadwheel – the hand-cranked hard-labour machine (see 3 December, p. 180). Not all such labour was wasted here, as some hand cranks pumped water from the prison well or ground flour for use in the prison kitchens. The majority of male convicts picked oakum, while the female prisoners were kept gainfully occupied in the prison laundry. When the prison commissioners took over the prison in 1877, Wandsworth was adopted as a short-term prison. The prison took over execution duties for the south of London after the closure of Horsemonger Lane Gaol in 1878. Wandsworth remains a prison to this day (and maintained the last set of working gallows in the country until comparatively recent times).

22 August 1887

Israel Lipski (21), an umbrella-stick maker, was executed for the murder of Miriam Angel. In his confession written the night before his execution, Lipski swore he only entered the room of Mrs Angel with the intention of robbery. He thought she had money in her room. Mrs Angel awoke, whereupon he struck her on the head and held her mouth closed. He had poison in his pocket and forced some of it down Mrs Angel's throat. She fainted and he took the rest but without effect. Hearing voices coming up the stairs, he crawled under the bed to hide but was discovered. Poor Mrs Angel did not recover and Lipski stood trial for murder. Found guilty and sentenced to death, he 'walked firmly' on to the scaffold. The trial had attracted much public attention and generated much anti-Semitism. When the black flag was hoisted, it was met with uncharacteristic cheers from the crowd and the cry of 'Lipski', became a term of derision and abuse used against Jews in the East End for years to come. This term of derision was allegedly used against Israel Schwartz by the man (possibly Jack the Ripper) he saw throwing 'Long Liz' Stride to the ground at Dutfield's Yard beside the International Working Men's Club on Berner Street at about 12.45 a.m. on 30 September 1888.

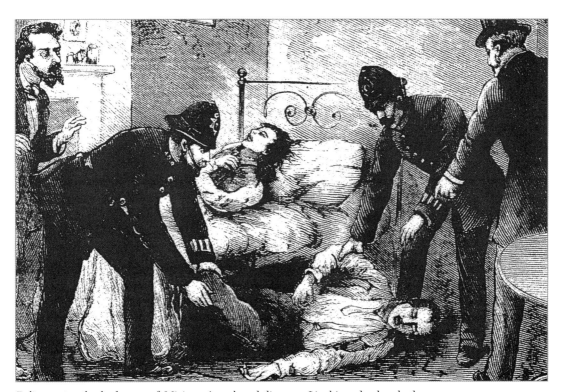

Police enter the bedroom of Miriam Angel and discover Lipski under her bed.

23 AUGUST Criminal Types: Sharpers

Another type warned of in late nineteenth-century London guides were 'sharpers'. Not just limited to three-card tricksters, 'sharpers' worked many varied fiddles to 'turn a few bob'. Among the scams were the 'ring dupe', where the innocent passer-by is induced to buy a worthless ring, purporting to be a diamond, from one who claims to have found it but claims he has neither time nor inclination to find a better market. There was the 'painted bird trick', whereby a worthless sparrow was painted or coloured and passed off as a valuable canary or piping bullfinch. There were even 'fly' horsedealers who would, by artful means, make worthless horses appear valuable and sell them, claiming that the sale was caused by the death of a relative. They gave every promise of fair trials and money back if not completely satisfied, but all such promises and paperwork were worthless.

24 AUGUST 1888

Barnet Levy (83), an elderly one-legged man who had to be carried into the dock of Worship Street Court, was charged with assault by striking Nathan Corber with his crutch. Levy sold matches about the streets and lived in Back Church Lane, Whitechapel. Corber, a pickler of Shepherd Street, Spitalfields, had seen Levy the previous afternoon putting a bottle into his pocket and had called to him, saying, 'Mind you don't drop it, Daddy.' Levy replied by delivering a blow with his crutch to Corber's head, catching his eye. A policeman was summoned. Levy stated he had been subjected to 'chaffing' or 'hooting' by Corber and complained, 'Boys are always annoying me.' The magistrate was unimpressed. Levy had been as awkward as possible: despite being perfectly able to walk with a crutch he had refused to walk since he had been taken into custody. Describing the assault as 'outrageous', and notwithstanding Levy's great age, he was sentenced to twenty-one days' imprisonment. The law report wryly concluded, 'The prisoner was carried out of the court.'

25 AUGUST 1879

James Dilley was executed at Newgate for the murder of his illegitimate child.

26 AUGUST 1883

The body of Ernest Benning (21) was laid out for identification at the Thames River Police mortuary. He and his pals Frank Palmer and Jeanette Simmonds had hired a boat from Waterloo Bridge the previous day and rowed to Kew where they had tea. The set off to row back at 7 p.m. and arrived at Pimlico at 9 p.m. Benning was far more interested in his conversation with Miss Simmonds than keeping an eye out for other river traffic in the darkening evening gloom. All at once a steamer loomed out of the darkness, the crew and passengers shouting a warning. The bow of the steamer struck the rowing boat and it capsized. All were rescued bar the love-struck Benning.

27 August 1888

An inquest was held at St Pancras Coroner's Court into the death of Louisa Minnie Fairservice (3½), whose parents resided at 25 Marsden Street, Kentish Town. Following the attestation of the surgeon and medical officer, it was concluded the little girl had died 'from exhaustion following enteric fever, probably caused by eating ices purchased in the street'. A strong recommendation was made that the sanitary authorities should be called upon to purchase ices from street vendors with a view to their being submitted for analysis to ascertain whether they contained anything injurious to health or not. In a previous analysis of 'street ices' or 'penny licks', otherwise known as 'hokey-pokey' in 1881, one sample was found to contain not only milk and water but an array of cotton fibres, straw, human and cat hairs, fleas, lice and bed bugs!

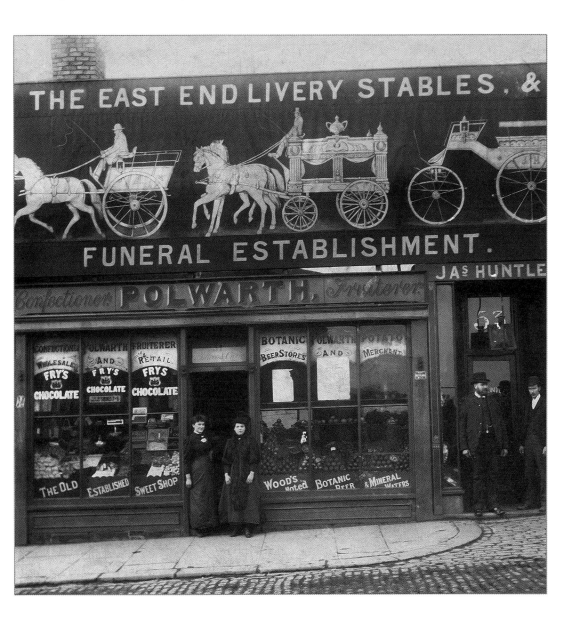

28 AUGUST Criminal Types: The Snide Pitcher

The snide pitcher is the man (or woman) who buys from or works in a team with the 'coiner' (see 10 August, p. 121) to pass forged coinage or 'bad money' as genuine. A typical scenario saw a well-dressed couple armed with a purse full of good coins but one 'snide'. Selecting shops with very young or elderly staff, the woman would enter and attempt to 'pass' the coin with a small and simple purchase, receiving genuine money in change, while her male partner kept lookout. If there was a query, it was hoped that the lady pitcher could simply claim she had been duped elsewhere and prove it by showing that the rest of her coins were real! If the pass had been successful, she would walk out, meet her male lookout and he would slip her another forged coin. As many as two dozen pieces of counterfeit money a day could be passed by the pitchers.

29 AUGUST 1876

John Ebelthrift, a labourer, was executed at Newgate. Ebelthrift and his wife, Emma, were both heavy drinkers; neighbours stated that arguments and mutual violence were common between them. On the fateful night Mrs Ebelthrift was talking to neighbours in front of her house on Clarendon Street when her husband was observed leaving the house to go drinking. Over an hour later he returned worse for drink and muttering the usual threats against his wife. Mrs Ebelthrift knew what was in store and locked him out of the bedroom. He appeared to calm down after a while and she opened the door to him, but soon a full-scale row erupted in which Ebelthrift held his wife down and stabbed her to death. Ebelthrift was soon in custody, stood trial, was found guilty of murder and sentenced to death. Sentence was carried out on this day by public executioner William Marwood.

30 AUGUST 1888

Fire broke out at the Shadwell Dry Dock, but was not brought under control until the following morning. Fires always drew hundreds of spectators, especially from the nearby East End. On this night the sky was stained red by the raging fire and many folks scuttled along the back alleys and roads to watch the horse-drawn steam fire engines with shiny brass boilers and streaming hoses struggle to contain and quench the conflagration. Policemen were thus distracted from their normal beats by the pressing duties of crowd control. Many subsequent witnesses at the inquests into the Jack the Ripper murders would remember their whereabouts by recalling where they were on the night of the dock fire.

31 AUGUST 1888

The first victim of the Whitechapel Murderer? The body of Mary Ann 'Polly' Nichols (43) was discovered at approximately 3.40 a.m. by carman Charles Cross as he turned into Buck's Row. He was soon joined by another carman, Robert Paul, who was also on his

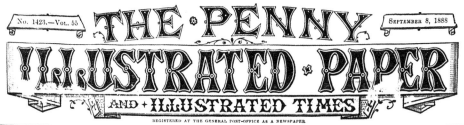

No. 1423.—Vol. 55

SEPTEMBER 8, 1888

THE · PENNY
ILLUSTRATED · PAPER
AND ·ILLUSTRATED TIMES

REGISTERED AT THE GENERAL POST-OFFICE AS A NEWSPAPER.

London : Printed and Published at the Office, 10, Milford-lane, Strand, in the Parish of St. Clement Danes, in the County of Middlesex, by Thomas Fox, 10, Milford-lane, Strand, aforesaid

P.C. NIEL J. 97.   DR LLEWELLYN   INSPR HELSON   THE CORONER

SKETCHES AT THE INQUEST

...ast London has a ...rror that must be ...amped out. We ...lustrate on this page, ...nd describe in ...other, Police-Con- ...able Niel's discovery ...murdered Mary Ann Nicholls in Buck's-row, Whitechapel, ...n the early morning of August the Thirty-first. This crime ...as so many points of similarity with the murders of the two ...her women in the same neighbourhood—one, Martha Turner, ...recently as Aug. 7, and the other less than twelve months ...reviously—that the police admit their belief that the three crimes are the ...ork of one individual. All three women were of the same class, and each of ...em was so poor that robbery could have formed no motive for the crime.

The Penny Illustrated Paper reflects the concern over the recent slaying on Buck's Row and makes it the cover story with a dramatic depiction of PC John Neil 97J discovering the body of Polly Nichols in the beam of his bull's-eye lamp. *(Stewart P. Evans)*

Dr Rees Ralph Llewellyn, the first doctor to examine Polly Nichols.

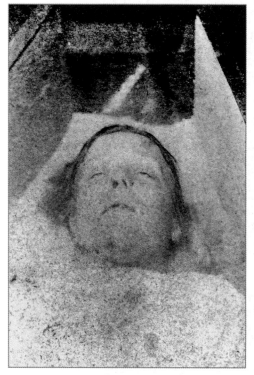

Mortuary photograph of Polly Nichols, the first widely accepted victim of Jack the Ripper. (*Stewart P. Evans*)

way to work. They concluded she was probably a rape victim still suffering concussion from her assault and went to summon a policeman. Cross and Paul encountered PC Mizen of H Division at the junction of Hanbury Street and informed him of what they had found. At the same time as they encountered Mizen, PC John Neil 97J was on patrol on Buck's Row, Whitechapel. At 3.45 a.m. he came across the body of Polly Nichols. Shortly after the grisly discovery, Neil heard PC Thaine on Brady Street and he called out, 'Run for Dr Llewellyn – a woman's been murdered.' Dr Rees Ralph Llewellyn was summoned to the scene and ordered the removal of the body to the mortuary. Her body was lifted on to the hand-wheeled ambulance by PCs Neil and Mizen and, accompanied by Sergeant Kirby, they trundled the mortal remains of Polly Nichols through the streets to the mortuary in Old Montague Street. Dr Llewellyn's examination findings are recorded in the Metropolitan Police Special Report compiled by Inspector Spratling and Supt Keating: '. . . her throat had been cut from left to right . . . windpipe, gullet and spinal cord being cut through . . . abdomen had been (cut) open from centre of bottom of ribs along right side, under pelvis to left of the stomach.' She had been disembowelled and received two small stabs 'on private parts'. She had last been seen at about 2.30 a.m. by Emily Holland, her friend from the Thrawl Street dosshouse, on the corner of Osborn Street and Whitechapel Road as she staggered off in a drunken state to earn her 4*d* doss money. As she left she called out, 'Never mind, I'll soon get my doss money. Look what a jolly bonnet I've got now.' This is acknowledged by most modern Ripperologists to be the first killing by the Whitechapel Fiend, at the time the murders of Martha Tabram (7 August) and Emma Smith (3 April) were also ascribed by the press and some police officers to the killer who would later be nicknamed 'Jack the Ripper'.

SEPTEMBER

✝

More lurid front page revelations from the *Illustrated Police News*
after the 'Anbury Street 'orror! *(Stewart P. Evans)*

1 SEPTEMBER Tales from the Autumn of Terror

A suggestion for the protection of the women of Whitechapel and the apprehension of the murderer appeared in the *Pall Mall Gazette*: 'There are numbers of well-trained pugilists in Shoreditch and Whitechapel whoare, many of them, young, and in the custom in their profession, clean shaved. . . . Twenty game men of this class in women's clothing loitering about Whitechapel would have more chance than any number of heavy-footed policemen.'

2 SEPTEMBER 1882

A wanted poster and photograph of John Novitsky (right), a Russian wanted on warrant for stealing a number of bonds, was circulated by the Metropolitan Police. 'Age about 45, height 5ft 7ins; full beard and moustache fair; hair dark brown, going grey, slightly curled; dress grey trousers, black coat and waistcoat, supposed to have been a Russian Officer, and a correspondent for the *Moscow Gazette*. A reward of £100 is offered for information leading to this man's apprehension.'

3 SEPTEMBER 1878

The Princess Alice disaster. The *Princess Alice* was one of the most popular pleasure steamers on the Thames. She returned from Sheerness on the evening of 3 September 1878 loaded to the gunnels (overloaded by about 200 passengers for its official capacity of 500) with day-tripping Londoners. At Woolwich the iron-clad collier *Bywell Castle* (a vessel five times the weight of the *Princess Alice*) was en route to Newcastle to take coal on for shipment to Alexandria. For some reason Captain Grinstead of the *Princess Alice* suddenly changed course and the *Bywell Castle* could not manoeuvre away in time. Its bows hit the *Princess Alice* just forward of the starboard paddle box, almost cutting her in two. The *Princess* sank in less than four minutes. Over 640 people were drowned, and many bodies were never recovered. Recovered bodies earned their finder twelve shillings a carcass, and so the waters around Woolwich were filled with any small vessel the enterprising could get their hands on in the days after the accident. Many unseemly struggles and fights to recover the dead ensued. One of the Ripper victims, 'Long Liz' Stride, always keen on telling a fanciful story, claimed that her husband and two children (one of the children clutched in her daddy's arms) 'were taken from her' by this disaster. This tale was no doubt created to appeal to Victorian sentimentality and solicit charity rather than reflect the truth. It is thought the couple had parted as late as 1882 and that John Stride died in the Bromley Asylum for the sick in 1884.

Relatives attempt to identify family members from the bodies recovered after the *Princess Alice* disaster.

4 SEPTEMBER 1888

Press reports of the Whitechapel Murderer stated that the police were questioning slaughtermen. Notably, a man known in the Whitechapel area as 'Leather Apron' (John Pizer) was wanted for questioning in connection with the Whitechapel murders because of his reputation for 'ill-using prostitutes'.

5 SEPTEMBER Prisons and Punishments

One of the oldest traditions of the London prisons was the 'Newgate Bell', which was tolled twelve times with double strokes as any condemned prisoner left Newgate on their final journey to the gallows at Tyburn. This tradition was maintained through the endowment of Robert Dow, a London merchant, who, in 1604, bequeathed £1 6s 8d a year for the sexton or bell-man of St Sepulchre's Church (opposite Newgate) to toll the bell accordingly. Originally the sexton was also required to ring a handbell outside the prison at midnight and exhort a standard tract to implore all within to search their souls and repent their sins. The handbell and ex-hortation tradition did not endure but the tolling bell did. Even after executions were removed behind prison walls in 1868, the bell began to strike at the appointed hour when the condemned prisoner left his cell to proceed to the execution shed. In September 1888 Robert

'Bird Cage Walk' otherwise known as 'The Graveyard' at Newgate Prison. The primary purpose of this passageway is to provide a secure route from the prison to The Old Bailey. The warnings were literally on the wall because a number of the blocks of stone down here bore simply the surname initial of prisoners executed and buried under the very flagstones the reader was standing on!

owe's charity was recognised by the charity commissioners and was noted for its benevolence towards providing clothing for juvenile offenders and aiding prisoners discharged from the Central Criminal Court district. After strict observance for 286 years, a request was made to the vicar of St Sepulchre's that the bell not be tolled for the execution of Mary Pearcey (see 23 December, p. 188) in 1890 on account of a guest at the nearby Viaduct Hotel being seriously ill. The bell was not tolled and never rang for another execution.

6 SEPTEMBER 1888

John McCarthy was one of three charioteers taking part in a display in the grand arena of the Italian Exhibition. McCarthy was driving a chariot pulled by two magnificent black horses. In turning the corner near the Emperor's box, the chariot tilted and then righted itself, throwing McCarthy on to the ground. Mr Knowles, who was following close behind in the second chariot, pulled the reigns to the offside so hard he broke the splinter bar of the chariot and was also thrown to the ground. The near wheel of Knowles's uncontrolled chariot passed over the right side of McCarthy's body. Despite being rapidly removed to the West London Hospital he was pronounced dead on arrival.

7 SEPTEMBER 1889

A strange coincidence? A man who gave his name as John Cleary went to the London offices of the *New York Herald* on the morning of the 8th, claiming that Jack the Ripper had struck again on Back Church Lane. Cleary stated the body had been found by a policeman at about 11.20 p.m. on the 7th. Reporters went rushing down but found no evidence of the crime, and when they did find an inspector, it was news to him that any crime had been committed. This incident was shrugged off as one of many hoax calls inspired by the Ripper hyperbole. Then, on 10 September, a human torso was discovered on Pinchin Street, the street that runs directly on from the end of Back Church Lane! Discovered by a chance sweep of PC Pennett's bull's-eye lamp, the torso was lying some 18ft from the main roadway. The head and legs had been removed but the arms remained. The only item of clothing was a torn chemise positioned over her neck and right shoulder. A search for Cleary, the man who went to the *Herald* offices revealed him to be a news vendor named John Arnold, but he stuck by his story. The body was never positively identified, her killer was never caught and quite what happened on the night of 7 September 1889 remains unresolved.

8 SEPTEMBER 1888

The second victim. The body of Annie Chapman (a.k.a. Siffey) (47), commonly known as 'Dark Annie', was found at about 6 a.m. by John Davis, an elderly lodger at 29 Hanbury Street in the back yard in the recess between the backyard steps and the fence. Her head was facing towards the house and she had been horribly mutilated. Davis ran out on to Hanbury Street to raise the alarm and then on to the Commercial Street police station. Inspector Chandler was on duty and raced to the scene. He later compiled a special report which stated that Annie Chapman had been found, 'Lying on her back, dead, left arm resting on left breast, legs drawn up . . . intestines and flap of abdomen lying on right side, above right shoulder attached by a cord . . . two flaps of skin from the lower part of the abdomen lying in a large quantity of blood above the left shoulder; throat cut deeply from left and back in a jagged manner right around throat.' As the news got out crowds came to view the body and site of the killing; local residents charged a penny to look out of the windows of adjoining properties with views of the back-yard murder scene. Police found two misleading 'clues' in the back-yard, a fragment of an envelope bearing the crest of the Royal Sussex Regiment with two white pills nearby and a freshly washed leather apron about 2ft away from the water tap. Rumours became rife. Was the murderer a slaughterhouse worker, a butcher or anyone who wore a leather apron, such as a cobbler or cork worker? Another foul rumour circulated that the killer had scrawled 'Five, fifteen more and then I give myself up' on the fence above poor Annie.

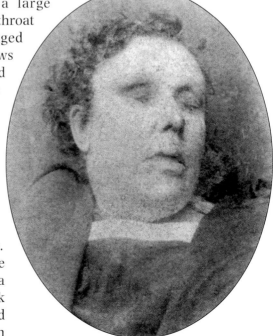

Mortuary photograph of Annie Chapman. *(Stewart P. Evans)*

The *Illustrated Police News* luridly resplendent with the latest news of the Whitechapel Murderer and his latest victim, Annie Chapman. *(Stewart P. Evans)*

9 September 1888

Regarding the Whitechapel Murderer . . . The following letter was received by the editor of *The Times*:

> Sir, – I would suggest that the police should at once find out the whereabouts of all cases of 'homicidal mania' which may have been discharged as 'cured' from metropolitan Asylums during the last two years.
>
> Your obedient servant
> A COUNTRY DOCTOR

10 September 1888

Dissatisfied with police progress and concerned for the safety of the people of the East End, a disparate body of interested parties from tradesmen to labourers gathered at the Crown public house on Mile End Road to form the Whitechapel Vigilance Committee. At a meeting convened on this day, local vestryman George Lusk was appointed their chairman and Joseph Aarons, the licensee of the Crown, to be their treasurer. This was a day for decisive action by the police. John 'Leather Apron' Pizer, a man known for abusing prostitutes, was arrested by Sergeant Thick and several sharp, long-bladed knives were found on his premises at 22 Mulberry Street. Pizer was taken to Leman Street police station. His friends confirmed his alibis and he was released the following day, but still the broadsheets demanded the capture of 'Leather Apron', which was no longer a name just for Pizer but a generic term for the Whitechapel Murderer, who was thought to be a slaughterman or tradesman skilled with his knife, such as a cork worker or cobbler. Meanwhile Detective Inspector Abberline drew a crowd at Commercial Street police station. He had arrived hotfoot from Gravesend with a suspect, one William Piggott. Piggott was apprehended for being seen drinking in a pub wearing a bloodstained shirt. He was known in Gravesend for his strange behaviour, but he was not identified by police witnesses. Within two hours his speech had become so garbled that a doctor was sent for to assess his sanity. Piggott was pronounced insane and immediately removed to the asylum at Bow.

11 September 1875

The dismembered body of a woman, wrapped in two parcels of American cloth was discovered in a hansom cab with an actress and respectable local businessman. The cab was occupied by pretty Whitechapel Pavilion chorus girl Violet Dash, who had been offered a ride by philanthropic local businessman Henry Wainright. The cab was stopped in Borough High Street by a police officer who had been alerted by Alfred Stokes, a Wainwright employee, who had suspicions about the parcels when Wainwright had picked them up from his Vine Court warehouse. Although he was offered £100 to just go away, the policeman persisted to know what was in the parcels. The dismembered body of a woman was soon revealed and Miss Dash and Wainwright were taken into custody. Miss Dash was soon found to have no connection with the horrific discovery and released but Wainwright was detained 'for further questioning'. Wainwright was seen

'What's this you got wrapped up here, Mr Wainwright?' *(Stewart P. Evans)*

by many as a respectable man, churchwarden, husband and father of four children, but enquiries soon revealed he had another family living between his home and brush-making warehouse. Here he lived with Harriet Lane and their two children as Mr and Mrs King. Because of financial difficulties, he cut Harriet's allowance, moved her to cheaper accommodation and sent the children to stay with friends. Harriet went to the warehouse to complain but when this became a row Wainwright shot and battered her to death. He hid the body in the warehouse but bankruptcy forced him to move it. Wainwright's brother Thomas assisted with the dismemberment. Wainwright's brother was given seven years' hard labour for his complicity, whereas Wainwright himself went to the gallows on 21 December. The case was a public sensation and over eighty 'guests' were invited to the execution at Newgate. A nasty piece to the end, Wainwright discarded his cigar as he approached the gallows and called to those assembled, 'Come to see a man die, have you, you curs?'

12 SEPTEMBER 1888

Jacob Isenschmid arrested. Following concerns expressed by Drs Cowan and Crabb to the police at Holloway on 11 September about a certain Jacob Isenschmid, Detective Inspector Styles was sent to investigate this potential Jack the Ripper suspect. Once in custody Isenschmid was soon certified a lunatic and sent under restraint to Islington Workhouse and later the Grove Hall Lunatic Asylum. Isenschmid was still in medical care when 'Long Liz' Stride and Mary Kelly were murdered.

13 SEPTEMBER Tales from the Autumn of Terror

The streets of the East End were still buzzing with stories of the 'anbury Street 'orror. Such was the speed with which the horror travelled that within hours of the murder a broadsheet of doggerel verses entitled 'Lines on the Terrible Tragedy' was being hawked on the streets by long-song sellers who cried out the verses to the hardly appropriate tune of 'My Village Home'. Following the repeated assertion in the press and on the streets that 'no Englishman could have perpetrated such a horrible crime', there were numerous cases of assault upon 'foreign types', especially on members of the East End Jewish population. The *Daily News* expanded the story to claim that the divisional police surgeon (George Bagster Phillips) and his assistant were 'out of their beds nearly all Saturday night on cases of assault'. The paper sensationally concluded that 'there may soon be murders from panic to add to murders from lust for blood . . . a touch will fire the whole district, in the mood which it is now'.

14 SEPTEMBER 1877

Alfred Park had returned in his usual drunken state to his wife Elizabeth at their lodgings on George Street, Stepney. One of their frequent rows erupted. Although Park had previously been fined £5 for assaulting her, he drew a knife from his sleeve and he said he 'meant to do for her'. Elizabeth ran out of their house and into the door of No. 31 where the landlady, Elizabeth Wood, saw Park strike and kick his wife twice. PC Richard Talbot 102K intervened and Park ran off. He was apprehended and appeared before the court the next day. Found guilty of the assault on his wife, Park was sentenced to three months' hard labour.

15 SEPTEMBER 1884

The death of 'Champagne Charlie'. One of the most popular songs of late Victorian England was 'Champagne Charlie', a song popularised by George Leybourne who trod the boards of London music halls immaculately turned out in tails and top hat evening wear and sporting a monocle. He was the archetypal 'tipsy gent'. The tragedy was that most of the time he was not acting. Having squandered all his money on drink, he died lonely and penniless at his Islington home. He is buried in Abney Park, Stoke Newington, under the epitaph 'God's finger touched him and he slept.'

16 SEPTEMBER 1889

An inquest was held at Charing Cross Hospital on the body of Walter Overy Cleverley (13), an office boy in the service of the Discount Banking Company, son of PC William Cleverley of B Division. It appeared that Mr Lewis Simmons, the banker, kept a revolver in his drawer in the event of a robbery. Simmons left George Hester, his chief clerk and two of the office boys, Cleverley and Walter George, in charge over lunchtime. Hester popped out and the boys nipped into Simmons's office to find the revolver they knew he kept there. They started 'larking about' and it went off. The inquest recorded a verdict of 'accidental death'.

17 September 1877

An inquest was held at Buffalo's Head, Marylebone Road, on the body of Samuel Hutchins (16). It was deposed that the boy helped his mother, who was a muffin baker, between 3 a.m. and 8 a.m. At 8.30 a.m. the boy then went to work at Balls & Co., upholsterers, where he worked until 8.30 p.m. – a total of seventeen hours of work a day! The boy had been found dead in the bedding room with a window sash line round his neck but there was no evidence to show how it got there. Alfred Bull, a dusting boy, said Hutchins had told him he had been to theatres and could show him how they hung people there; it was also stated at the inquest that the deceased 'was in the habit of reading low-class magazines of the penny dreadful type'. The cause of death was given as strangulation and an open verdict was recorded.

18 September 1888

PC John Johnson (number 866 of the City force) was on duty in the Minories at about three o'clock in the morning when he heard loud screams of 'Murder' from a dark court. Running towards the screams, Johnson found it led to Butcher's Row and some railway arches near Whitechapel Road, where he found a man behaving in threatening manner with a prostitute named Elizabeth Burns. Asked what he was doing, the man replied 'nothing', but the distressed 'unfortunate' begged, 'Oh, policeman, do take me out of this.' PC Johnson sent the man on his way and walked with the woman, who was too shaken to speak properly, to the end of his beat, when she blurted out, 'Dear me, he frightened me very much when he pulled that big knife out.' The constable set out in pursuit of the man but he could not be found. The man was apprehended at about 3 a.m. after an altercation at a coffee stall, where he drew a knife and threatened Alexander Finlay (also known as Freinburg). PC John Gallagher 221H intervened and arrested the man subsequently identified as German immigrant Charles Ludwig. Ludwig was held for a fortnight until his hearing at Thames Magistrates Court. Being in custody at the time of the murders of Stride and Eddowes, Ludwig was thus provided with solid alibis for the latest Ripper killings. Magistrates considered he had been incarcerated enough for his crimes and released him.

19 September 1888

An inquest was held at the City Mortuary into the death of Mr G.H. Hall, a brewer of Beckenham. It transpired Hall had had 'business worries'. He had purchased three separate bottles of a patent medicine named 'Chloral' and gone to the City

Central Hotel. He was discovered dead in his bed the following day. An examination of the medicine revealed that each bottle contained about 180 grains of chloral, a full sleeping dose being 30 grains. The jury returned a verdict of suicide while temporarily insane and recommended steps should be taken to prevent the ready sale of chloral. On this same day Sir Charles Warren sent a report to the Home Office discussing the suspects Isenschmid (which Warren spells Isensmith) (see 12 September, p. 138) and Oswald Puckeridge, of whom Warren states he was 'released from an asylum on 4th August. He was educated as a surgeon – he has threatened to rip people up with a long knife. He is being looked for but cannot be found yet.' Finally, he notes, ' A Brothel Keeper who will not give her address or name writes to say that a man living in her house was seen with blood on him on the morning of the murder . . . when the detectives came near him he bolted, got away and there is no clue to the writer of the letter.'

20 SEPTEMBER 1888

John Bunyan (40), a brass-finisher, pleaded guilty at the Central Criminal Court to throwing vitriol (a highly corrosive fluid) at Henrietta Casey. Bunyan and Casey had lived together but she had had enough of his bad moods and drinking, and found other lodgings. Bunyan met Casey at Victoria. After walking and talking with him for some distance, she told him to go. He drew back her hair as if to caress her and threw the corrosive liquid in her face, causing 'much burning'. Bunyan pleaded passion in the heat of drunkenness but the bottle of vitriol in his pocket proved the intent of the crime. Bunyan was sentenced to eighteen months with hard labour.

21 SEPTEMBER 1892

This was the opening day at the Central Criminal Court of the trial of John James Banbury (22), who was charged with the murder of Miss Emma Oakley. The case was quite simple. Banbury had gone out for the day in a cab driven by an acquaintance named Briggs. They stopped to booze in pubs when Briggs was desirous of changing his horse. At one point Banbury told him to wait and he would soon return. Banbury then walked smartly round to Grosvenor Park where Emma Oakley lived. They had been 'walking out' for some time but turned him down when Banbury proposed and said she had feelings for another. The housekeeper at Oakley's house heard the report of a firearm, and, looking out of the window, soon saw Banbury leaving the house putting something in his pocket. She found the young lady lying on the floor near the window in the front parlour fatally wounded with gunshots. When the surgeon examined her body he found four bullet wounds in the head and neck. Banbury bragged to Briggs when they went for a drink that he had just shot his girl: 'I love her and I swore no one else should have her.' The first trial of Banbury ended in farce when it transpired that two of the jurymen were deaf. He was tried again and found guilty. Sentenced to death, Banbury met his end on the Wandsworth gallows at the hands of Public Executioner James Billington on 11 October 1892.

Central Criminal Court in session, *c.* 1888.

22 SEPTEMBER 1888

Mr Wynne E. Baxter, coroner for the South-Eastern Division of Middlesex, resumed the adjourned inquest into the murder of Mary Ann 'Polly' Nichols at the Working Lad's Institute, Whitechapel Road. Dr Llewellyn stated the injuries on Nichols 'could have been produced by a long-bladed instrument moderately sharp'. Dr Phillips commented on the Chapman murder where the injuries 'were by a very sharp knife, probably with a thin, narrow blade, at least 6in. to 8in. in length, probably longer.' Comment was made on the considerable similarity of the injuries in both murders. One of the most contentious and debated statements in the crime ensued, it being suggested that the injuries 'in each case been performed with anatomical knowledge'.

23 SEPTEMBER 1888

The stolen kiss. Edward Gascoigne Hawkes (25), a solicitor's clerk of gentlemanly appearance, appeared at Worship Street Court charged with having assaulted Alice Farrell by kissing her in the carriage of a GER train. Miss Farrell, a waitress in the employ of the Aerated Bread Company, knew Hawkes by sight and encountered him on her way home to Leyton, Essex. They boarded the train at Liverpool Street together. She claimed that as soon as the train pulled away Hawkes's arms were around her waist and he started kissing her. She pulled away but he would not stop until she punched him and dragged herself out of the carriage at the first stop, Bishopgate, where the incident was reported to the guard. Hawkes admitted to putting his arm around her waist but not to kissing her. The magistrate ordered the prisoner to pay a fine of £5 or go to prison for ten days with hard labour. The fine was paid.

24 SEPTEMBER Tales from the Autumn of Terror

Never one to miss a chance to publicise the plight of his flock, Canon Samuel Barnett (1844–1913) of St Jude's and founder warden of Toynbee Hall wrote an extended letter to *The Times* (published on 19 September 1888). His arguments were clear: there should be a national effort to rehouse the poor because such was degradation in which many in the End End lived, especially in Spitalfields, that crime was an inevitability. Part of his letter stated, 'Whitechapel horrors will not be in vain, if "at last" public conscience awakes to consider the life which these horrors reveal. The murders were, it may also be said, bound to come; generation could not follow generation in lawless intercourse . . .'

Canon Samuel Barnett.

He then made four practical suggestions, namely, (1) efficient police supervision, (2) adequate lighting and cleaning, (3) the removal of slaughterhouses (such sights as blood on the streets from the butchers and slaughterhouses 'brutalise ignorant natures'), and (4) the control of tenement houses by responsible landlords. There was no groundswell from the government or the people of Britain to improve the lot of the poverty-stricken in the East End, but Canon Barnett never lost hope and, tirelessly working with local councils, charities and benevolent individuals and organisations, did much to improve the life of many in the hardest quarters of the East End.

25 SEPTEMBER Criminal Types: The 'Pimp', 'Ponce' or 'Bully'

As ex-Detective Superintendent John Gosling and Douglas Warner eloquently put it in *The Shame of a City: An Enquiry into the Vice of London*, 'One of the many fallacies about prostitution is that the male pimp (or 'ponce' or 'bully') is a universal phenomenon wherever prostitutes are to be found. . . . Although parasites of one sort or another are to be found living off harlot's earnings in all civilisations and in all nuances of harlotry, the male pimp did not become ubiquitous in London until after 1885.' They really came into their own after the legislation that made running brothels impossible was passed and consequently affected the way prostitutes lived and worked. For instance, two working girls could not even share a rented room to live and sleep, and although they were able to take clients back to rooms, they could not be as blatant as before because punishments for lodging-house keepers were stiff. Many girls simply took to the streets to conduct their business, and soon, following threats, increasingly serious assaults and knifings, the pimps saw their chance and carved up areas of Whitechapel in which they would demand money for 'protection' from the girls working as prostitutes in that area. One of the most notorious gangs in the Whitechapel area were the Hoxton High Rips gang. Although they may have seen off a few drunks who were behaving aggressively towards the girls, the main use of their threats and coercion was directed towards the girls in the collection of their 'dues'.

26 September 1888

John Fitzgerald gave himself up to the police claiming to be the murderer of Annie Chapman. A statement was taken and investigated. It soon emerged Fitzgerald had a cast-iron alibi and could not have committed the crime. Given a stern warning about wasting police time, he was released on 29 September.

27 September 1888

Red letter day. This date was postmarked on the letter received at the offices of the Central News Agency, New Bridge Street, Ludgate Circus. Posted in EC1 (East London), it read:

Dear Boss.
I keep on hearing the police have caught me but they wont fix me just yet. I have laughed when they look so clever and talk about being on the right track. That joke about Leather Apron gave me real fits. I am down on whores and I shant quit ripping them till I do get buckled. Grand work the last job was, I gave the lady no time to squeal. How can they catch me now. I love my work and want to start again. You will soon hear of me with my funny little games. I saved some of the proper red stuff in a ginger beer bottle over the last job to write with but it went thick like glue and I cant use it. Red ink is fit enough I hope ha ha. The next job I do I shall clip the ladys ears off and send to the police officers just for jolly wouldn't you. Keep this letter back till I do a bit more work then give it out straight. My knife's so nice and sharp I want to get to work right away if I get a chance. Good luck.
  Yours truly
  Jack the Ripper

Don't mind me giving the trade name. Wasn't good enough to post this before I got all the red ink off my hands curse it. No luck yet. They say I'm a doctor now ha ha.

This lurid missive would come to be known as the 'Dear Boss' letter, and it was more likely to have been penned by an unscrupulous journalist hoping to add yet another twist to the tale than the actual murderer. The theme took off and soon hundreds of letters were being sent to London and provincial police forces and civic officials purporting to come from the Whitechapel Murderer. This letter, however, remains unique and has gone down in infamy as the first appearance of the name 'Jack the Ripper'.

28 September 1889

An inquest was held at St Pancras Coroner's Court before Dr G. Danford Thomas into the death of Thomas Lloyd (23), an engine cleaner in the employ of the LNWR at Camden Goods Station. It appeared a steam engine and eight or ten trucks were picking up ballast in front of the locomotive shed where Lloyd was working with another man named William Anderson. The gates of the shed were open and the engine moved the trucks up to clear the points, blowing its whistle and the ballast guard checking all was clear before doing so. Anderson noticed Lloyd was caught between the buffers of the engine and a ballast truck. Lloyd was extricated but was quite dead. The same statement came out again and again from the witnesses: when engaged in cleaning work in sheds men should not have to look out for shunting work. The foreman of the jury said he was an engine cleaner on the Midland Railway and if such practices were allowed 'none of the men's lives would be worth much' owing to the lack of lookouts. It was also pointed out that if the gates of the shed had been closed, the accident would probably not have happened, because the gates would have been damaged and guards knew for such an error they would be fined or suspended. A verdict of accidental death was passed.

29 September 1888

Charles Carver appeared on remand at Lambeth Police Court for begging. Carver had been spotted in the Denmark Hill area with some printed pamphlets relating to the Whitechapel murders. He was frequently seen to press the papers between his hands and 'pray that persons might be saved from cutting up'. When he was given money he would pour out blessings on the giver, especially, 'Those who give to the poor lend to the Lord.' When refused he would expound a stream of foul language and call people 'servants of the Devil'. Exposed as a rank impostor, he was sentenced to three months' hard labour.

30 September 1888

Double event. At 12.45 a.m. Israel Schwartz followed a man who appeared to be drunk into Berner Street from Commercial Road. As the man walked along the road, he was seen by Schwartz to stop and speak with a woman later identified as Elizabeth Stride. He then threw her to the ground and attempted to drag her into Dutfield's Yard beside the International Workmen's Club. She screamed three times, but not very loudly. Schwartz wanted no part of this strife and crossed to the other side of the road where he

POLICE NOTICE.

TO THE OCCUPIER.

On the mornings of Friday, 31st August, Saturday 8th, and Sunday, 30th September 1888, Women were murdered in or near Whitechapel, supposed by some one residing in the immediate neighbourhood. Should you know of any person to whom suspicion is attached, you are earnestly requested to communicate at once with the nearest Police Station.

Metropolitan Police Office
30th September 1888

Printed by McCorquadale & Co. Limited, "The Armoury," Southwark

Police notice seeking information about the Whitechapel murders ironically published on the day of the 'Double Event'.

Press coverage of the 'Double Event of 30 September 1888.
Mortuary photograph of Elizabeth Stride. *(Stewart P. Evans)*

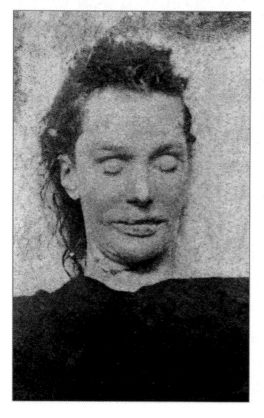

saw a man lighting his pipe. The man who threw the woman down could see Schwartz was staring and he shouted the typical abusive name for East End Jews at the time, 'Lipski' (see 22 August, p. 125). The man who lit his pipe began to follow Schwartz, so Schwartz ran off. Later that night, at 1 a.m. Louis Diemshutz was returning to Dutfield's Yard with his costermonger's barrow when his pony shied and would not walk on. Diemshutz went to investigate and saw what he thought was a pile of old clothes lying in the yard. He struck a match that was almost instantly blown out by the wind, but he had seen enough to know it was a corpse. It was the dead body of a prostitute named Elizabeth Stride, commonly known as 'Long Liz'. Her throat had been slashed across, but she had not been mutilated – many drew the conclusion that Jack had been disturbed. If Jack had not had his hideous appetite for mutilation sated, he soon found a second victim to satisfy it.

The hideously mutilated body of Catherine 'Kate' Eddowes (a.k.a. Kelly) was found on City Police territory in Mitre Square, Aldgate, by City PC Edward Watkins 881 at 1.45 a.m. Her throat had been slashed across, her face marked with quite deliberate cuts, her insides laid open and most of her womb, bladder and kidney removed. Tragically, Eddowes had been in police custody at Bishopgate Police Station for drunkenness on Aldgate High Street until 1 a.m., and had left with a cheery 'Goodnight old cock' when she was discharged. Major Henry Smith, Acting Police Commissioner for the City of London force, was summoned to the scene from the police station on Cloak Lane. He was to claim in his memoirs that they were so close on the killer's heels that a sink on Dorset Street was found to still have blood swirling in it where the Ripper had stopped to wash his hands. This night of macabre events was concluded with a discovery made by PC Alfred Long of H Division in the doorway of 108–19 Wentworth Model Dwellings, Goulston Street. It was a piece of material torn from

Kate's apron and smeared with blood and faeces, with which the murderer had probably wiped his knife and hands. Above it, written 'in a good schoolboy hand' was the statement, 'The Juwes are the men that will not be blamed for nothing.' Sir Charles Warren attended the scene in person and personally gave a direct order to 'obliterate the writing at once'. No doubt fearing riots and reprisals against the Jewish population in the East End if such an inflammatory statement became popular knowledge, and rather than wait until there was enough light to photograph the message, he controversially overruled the other officers on the scene and only had the message copied. Some accounts even claim Warren erased the message himself.

OCTOBER

✠

Sketches from the *Penny Illustrated Paper* of Kate Eddowes, the Mitre Square victim, her funeral and a suspicious character who visited George Lusk, the chairman of the Whitechapel Vigilance Committee.

1 OCTOBER 1888

A postcard smeared with blood and written in red ink was received by the Central News Agency. Its contents immortalised the previous night's atrocities as 'The Double Event': 'I was not codding dear old Boss when I gave you the tip. You'll hear about saucy Jacky's work tomorrow. Double event this time. Number one squealed a bit. Couldn't finish straight off. Had not time to get ears for police. Thanks for keeping back the last letter till I got to work again – Jack the Ripper.'

2 OCTOBER 1888

Private Investigators Grand and Batchelor (employed by the Whitechapel Vigilance Committee) found a bloodstained grape stalk in a drain near where the body of Elizabeth Stride was found. This information was not widely broadcast but entered East End folklore when combined with the account of Matthew Packer (who ran a small greengrocer's through a street window at 44 Berner Street) that he had served a man accompanied by Elizabeth Stride with half a pound of black grapes. The grapes have taken on yet greater significance in recent years as imaginative theorists of the killer suggest he laced the grapes with laudanum to stupor his victims prior to his attack. Also on this day Robert James Lees, a medium, offered his powers as a psychic to assist the police. Lees recorded in his diary that he was 'called a fool and a lunatic'.

One of the window shops on Whitechapel High Street, *c.* 1888. It was from premises similar to this that Matthew Packer served the man he thought was the Whitechapel murderer with some grapes.

3 OCTOBER 1888

On this date it was reported that on the previous day workmen discovered a human torso in one of the cellars of the New Scotland Yard building on the Embankment. Upon examination, the trunk was found to be that of an adult female with her arms,

(Stewart P. Evans)

CANINE DETECTIVE MOVEMENT: SPITZBERGEN TERRIER DISCOVERING REMAINS AT WHITEHALL.

legs and head cut off. Only the arms, minus the hands, were later recovered from the Thames. The rest of the body parts were never found, the torso was never identified and the perpetrator of this dastardly deed was never caught. The capital's new police headquarters is therefore literally built on an unsolved mystery!

3 October 1899

Pure coincidence? Frederick Preston (22), a French polisher, was executed by James Billington at Newgate for the murder of his girlfriend, Eliza Mears. After they had been going out together for some time, Eliza's mother had suggested she give him up because of the way he treated her. Eliza explained the situation to Preston and he beat her to death in a drunken frenzy with a blunt instrument. Almost a year to the day, on 2 October 1900, John Charles Parr (19) was also executed by James Billington at Newgate for shooting his girlfriend near Bethnal Green Police station *after she had left him*. He had claimed to be a *French polisher*.

4 OCTOBER 1899

Robert Ward (27), a bricklayer of Boundary Lane, Walworth, was executed at Wandsworth Prison. Claiming he had been driven to commit this horrible crime 'through the worry of my wife', Ward murdered both his children, Margaret Florence (5) and Louisa (2), and then attempted to take his own life. Unsuccessful in his suicide, he was arrested, stood trial and sentenced to death.

5 OCTOBER 1885

Henry Norman (31) was executed at Newgate. Norman, a painter by trade, had become increasingly suspicious of the relationship between his wife, Ellen, and John Batten, the landlord of their lodgings at 10 Rylston Road, Fulham. Norman accused his wife of improper relations with Batten but she flatly denied the matter. Norman appeared to let his concerns drop, but it must have played on his mind and jealous paranoia for he stabbed her through the heart while she slept. When Batten was asked if he could think of any reason for Norman's actions, he said he could not think of any. At Norman's trial the jury didn't even retire to decide the verdict of guilty. The two Norman children were sent to the orphanage.

6 OCTOBER 1884

The double execution of Thomas Henry Orrock (21), a cabinet maker, and Thomas Harris (48), a market gardener, took place at Newgate. Although these men were executed together, they had committed very different crimes. Orrock, a regular member of the Baptist Chapel, Ashwin Street, Dalston, was out one night with two friends, and almost as a dare he said he would rob the chapel of its sacrament plate. Orrock's attempts to break into the chapel were frustrated by PC Cole, who caught Orrock while on his night patrol. A nasty fight ensued where Orrock drew his revolver and shot the young constable dead. Orrock was not caught until police received intelligence of his complicity in the crime while he was in prison on other, unrelated, charges. The case of Harris was far more prosaic. Harris had ill-treated his wife while under the influence of drink for years and had even suffered a prison term for his treatment of her. They regularly argued, until one day Harris totally lost control and cut his wife's throat. He claimed he had no recollection of the deed. Both men were found guilty and kept their appointment with executioner James Berry on this day. Both conducted themselves with fortitude. Orrock was led in first, prepared with restraints, cap and noose and waited on the trapdoors for Harris to be similarly prepared. A drop of 7ft 5in was allowed for both and with a push of the lever both men passed simultaneously to eternity. Dr Gilbert the prison surgeon and Mr S.F. Langham, the City Coroner agreed death had been instantaneous in both cases.

7 OCTOBER 1896

The newpapers reported the previous day's execution of James Jones (26) at Newgate. Jones, a ship's fireman, had stood trial at the Old Bailey for the murder of Edward White, whom he had stabbed to death after a quarrel. The newspapers recorded that he was contrite and that a reprieve had been applied for, but it transpired that Jones 'didn't want or expect one'. The execution was carried out by public executioner James Billington.

THE MURDER OF POLICE CONSTABLE COLE AT DALSTON.

MRS SHEPPARD SAW THE SHOTS FIRED

ELIZABETH BUCKNELL

RICHARD BUCKNELL HEARD THE SHOTS FIRED AND SAW THE STRUGGLE ON THE GROUND

MURDER £200 REWARD

PARDON

THOMAS HENRY ORROCK THE PRISONER

8 OCTOBER 1878

Thomas Smithers (31) was executed at Wandsworth House of Correction. A cook by trade, Smithers cohabited with Amy Judge at Battersea and had done her much good. Before her connection with Smithers, Judge had lived 'a very disreputable life'. When he discovered she had lapsed back to her old ways 'on the sly', he was seized by a fit of jealousy and murdered her. After sentence was passed Smithers collapsed in the dock and had to be carried from the courtroom. Enquiries were made into his state of mind but nothing came of it. He kept his appointment with Marwood the executioner, with a crowd of about 1,000 people amassed outside the prison to see the black flag raised to signify the sentence had been carried out.

9 OCTOBER 1888

With mounting pressure coming from all quarters for progress in tracking Jack the Ripper, any new ideas and methods which may have some merit were considered. (At this time there was little or no concept of using forensic clues to assist with detection.) On this day and the next Sir Charles Warren personally oversaw the trials of bloodhounds on Regent's Park. Two hounds, Barnaby and Burgho, were brought down to London from Scarborough by the well-known breeder, Mr Brough. Sir Charles even acted as quarry in one of the trials and expressed himself satisfied with the result. The incident did, however, acquire a certain mythology whereby both hounds and Sir Charles got lost in the London smog.

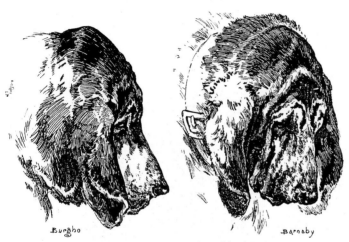

Burgho   Barnaby

The Bloodhounds used in the Trials.

10 OCTOBER 1888

George Richard Henderson, 'a man of singular appearance', appeared in court charged with 'being a suspicious person loitering about the streets'. About 3.30 a.m. the alarm had been raised at Covent Garden Market, where it was feared that Jack the Ripper was walking abroad and threatening people. Police were summoned and found Henderson 'behaving strangely . . . wandering about aimlessly carrying a black bag'. He was detained for not being able to give a proper account of himself, and when he was searched at the police station he was found to be carrying fifty-four different pawnbroker's tickets. Curiouser still, he was found to be carrying the rough draft of a letter to the Home Secretary, which had appeared in print, suggesting that those who were harbouring the Whitechapel murderer felt they were equally guilty as him because they were accomplices after the fact and could not come forward and give him up, no matter what the reward, until a free pardon was offered to them. Witnesses were called to the court and gave evidence as to Henderson's respectability. The bench agreed and Mr Vaughan the magistrate discharged Henderson, advising him not to go about the streets in a similar way again.

11 OCTOBER 1870

Margaret Walters (34) was executed at Horsemonger Lane for the murder of John Walter Cowen, an illegitimate child she had assumed the charge of for a consideration of money at her baby-farming establishment at 4 Frederick Terrace, Brixton. When she was first brought before the courts, Walters appeared with her sister, Sarah Ellis (23), on the same indictment. The case looked even worse when the bodies of emaciated babies were discovered near the trail of different addresses Walters and Ellis had stayed at. The evidence against Ellis apparently failed to support the capital charge so she was acquitted. She did, however, confess under her own volition to obtaining money by false pretences in connection with baby farming and was sentenced to eighteen months; hard labour. The full letter of the law was enacted against Walters. Protesting her innocence of intention to murder to the last, Margaret Walters went to the gallows unaided and without resistance, uttering 'a most touching and fervent prayer for forgiveness as the white cap and noose were adjusted'.

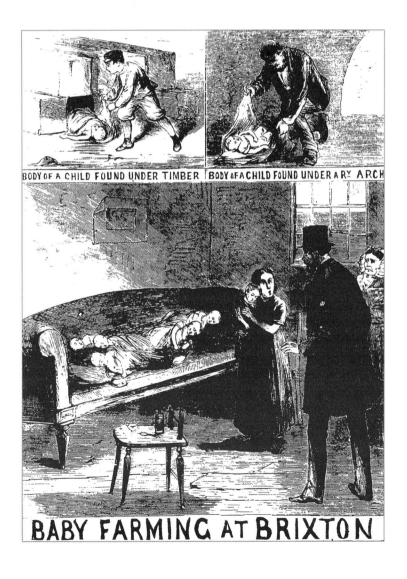

BODY OF A CHILD FOUND UNDER TIMBER | BODY OF A CHILD FOUND UNDER A RY ARCH

BABY FARMING AT BRIXTON

12 OCTOBER 1888

An American man named John Langan, who was in Boulogne seeking passage to South Wales to work in the mines, was brought to the attention of Police Assistant Commissioner Anderson by E.W. Bonham, HM Consul at Boulogne. The identification of Langan was based on, and a direct result of, the widely published line drawing and description of the man believed to be Jack the Ripper given by Matthew Packer, the Berner Street greengrocer who believed he had served Jack with grapes on the night of the 'Double Event' (see 30 September, p. 145). In order to stall him long enough for the London police to conduct enquiries he was detained on a charge of vagrancy by the French police. However, his American address and alibis proved valid and Langan was cleared and released on 16 November.

13 OCTOBER 1874

John Coppen was executed at Horsemonger Lane Gaol for the murder of his wife.

14 OCTOBER 1888

On and around this date the police started experiments with 'decoys' in attempts to draw out and capture the Ripper. Two clearly recorded decoys were Detective Sergeant Robinson, who took to the streets in 'veil, skirt and petticoats', and Detective Sergeant Mather, who remained in his plain clothes. While observing a man behaving in a strange manner with a woman in a doorway near Phoenix Place, St Pancras, the detectives were accused of being voyeurs by a passing cab washer named William Jarvis. Challenged with 'Wot yer muckin' about 'ere for?' the policemen identified themselves. 'Oh, a rozzer, eh?' Jarvis replied sceptically and belted Robinson in the eye. Another decoy was a volunteer named Amelia Brown of Peckham, who, although kept under close observation by policemen, was only issued with a police whistle for her personal protection.

15 OCTOBER Tales from the Autumn of Terror

Shortly after the Ripper's 'Double Event' on 30 September, a lurid pamphlet entitled 'The Curse of Mitre Square' began to be circulated on the streets of the East End. It stated that the square had been damned since the murder of another woman on exactly the same spot by a mad monk known as Brother Martin in 1530. (Mitre Square was indeed the site of the Priory of the Holy Trinity at that time.) The broadsheet maintained that a woman who was praying before the high altar was attacked by the insane monk. His knife 'descended with lightning rapidity, and pools of blood deluged the altar steps. With a demon's fury the monk then threw down the corpse and trod it out of recognition'. Brother Martin then plunged the knife into his own heart. The spot had remained unhallowed and the Ripper had simply fulfilled the ancient curse, or so the author of the broadsheet argued.

16 OCTOBER 1888

From Hell. George Lusk, chairman of the Whitechapel Vigilance Committee, received a small cardboard box wrapped in brown paper. To Lusk's horror, upon opening the parcel he found it contained a bloodstained letter and half a human kidney. The letter read thus:

> From Hell
>
> Mr Lusk
> Sir
>   I send you half the
> Kidne I took from one woman
> Preserved it for you, tother piece I
> fried and ate it was very nise. I
> may send you the bloody knife that
> took it out if you only wate a whil
> longer.
> signed Catch me when
>   you can
>   Mishter Lusk.

George Lusk, chairman of the Whitechapel Vigilance Committee. *(Leonard Archer)*

The kidney was examined by Dr Openshaw at the London Hospital, and he confirmed it was a longitudinally divided human kidney. Major Smith of the City Police added in his memoirs that 2in of the renal artery (averaging about 3in long) remained in Eddowes body where her kidney had been removed – 1in of artery was all that was attached to the organ sent to Lusk. (See 30 September, p. 145.)

17 OCTOBER 1888

An inquest was held by Coroner Wynne E. Baxter at the Vestry Hall, High Street, Shadwell, regarding the death of William Murgitroyd (64), a waterman. Alfred Cox, a fish porter from Bermondsey, deposed that he went to Murgitroyd at Tower Stairs and directed him to row him to Cherry Garden Pier. The current was strong so Murgitroyd asked Cox if he minded taking an oar. They had just got past Tower Bridge when Cox heard someone shout 'Look out!' Turning round, Cox saw the tug boat *Secret* about 15ft away and approaching fast. Before he had time to take evasive action, the tug struck the boat amidships. Cox grabbed the fender of the tug and was hauled aboard but he could not say exactly what happened to Murgitroyd. The tug even turned round to look for him, but he could not be found. John W. Lowe, the captain of the *Secret*, confirmed Cox's story and the inquest just returned a verdict of 'accidental death'.

The London Hospital on Whitechapel High Street, c. 1890.

18 OCTOBER Tales from the Autumn of Terror

During the month of October, the Victorian philanthropist Dr Thomas John Barnardo became involved in the story of Jack the Ripper. In an impassioned letter about the suffering of the children in common lodging houses to *The Times*, published on 9 October, he revealed the following: 'Only four days before the recent murders I visited No. 32 Flower and Dean Street, the house in which the unhappy woman Stride occasionally lodged. . . . In the kitchen of No. 32 there were many persons, some of them being girls and women of the same unhappy class as that to which poor Elizabeth Stride belonged. The company soon recognised me, and the conversation turned upon the previous murders. The female inmates of the kitchen seemed thoroughly frightened at the dangers to which they were presumably exposed. . . . One poor creature, who had evidently been drinking, exclaimed somewhat bitterly to the following effect:– "We're all up to no good, and no one cares what becomes of us. Perhaps some of us will be killed next!"' Barnardo continued: 'I have since visited the mortuary in which were lying the remains of the poor woman Stride, and I at once recognised her as one of those who stood around me in the kitchen of the common lodging-house on the occasion of my visit last Wednesday week.'

Women outside a Spitalfields lodging house on Flower and Dean Street.

19 OCTOBER Prisons and Punishments: The Fulham Refuge

The Fulham Refuge was opened in 1856; here there were places for 180 women close to release at the end of their sentences. If they had shown 'by their conduct whilst in the previous stages at Millbank and Brixton that they are inclined to profit by the instruction provided here', they were admitted to be trained in the skills of domestic servants. Following sporadic disturbances and a minor riot in 1864, the refuge had high walls topped with spikes built around it and greater discipline was phased in. By 1871 the refuge idea was abandoned in favour of a full-blown penitentiary. The site was expanded to accommodate 400 women and its name was changed to Fulham Prison. It closed in 1888 and the site was gradually demolished to make way for roads and houses. However, one building remains, the prison laundry, which was eventually converted into high-class private apartments.

20 OCTOBER 1888

Reports circulated of the death of Mrs Mary Burridge, a floor-cloth dealer on the Blackfriars Road. It was stated by some that she had been so overcome by reading a particularly lurid account of the Whitechapel Murders in the *Star* she fell dead, 'a copy of the late final in her hand'. Tom Cullen suggested in his *Jack the Ripper* that the following passage may have caught her eye: 'A nameless reprobate – half beast, half man – is at large. . . . Hideous malice, deadly cunning, insatiable thirst for blood – all these are the marks of the mad homicide. The ghoul-like creature, stalking down his victim like a Pawnee Indian, is simply drunk with blood, and he will have more.'

21 OCTOBER 1888

Maria Coroner (22), 'a respectable looking woman', appeared at Bradford Borough Court charged with writing 'certain letters tending to cause a breach of the peace . . . purported to be written by Jack the Ripper'. Appearing first on this day and refused bail until her second court appearance on the 24th, the message was clear to all – enough really was enough as far as the hoax letters were concerned. Shaken by the process of law she experienced, Miss Coroner was 'bound over in her own recognizance of £20 to be of good behaviour for 6 months'.

22 OCTOBER 1888

Reports were published of the inquest held at the Town Hall, Shoreditch, upon the body of Emily Roberts (43), wife of Joseph Roberts, a boot fitter, residing at 4 Essex Place, Hackney Road. According to Mr Roberts, he and his wife had 'had a few words' and she had knocked him down. He claimed he retaliated by striking her in the face, knocking her to the floor. The following day Mrs Roberts visited her niece, Emily Egling, who stated she saw her aunt's eyes were blackened and face bruised. She went on to state that her aunt said, 'He knocked me down last night and knelt on my stomach and hit me about the head. The quarrel was all over the cat.' Emily Roberts, daughter of Emily and Joseph, deposed that she saw her mother knock her father to the floor, but she swore she did not see her father kick her mother. Both niece and daughter admitted she 'had been in the habit of getting drunk' and that he knelt on her stomach when he hit her. Dr Robert Inman had been called to Emily the day after the assault and noted, 'She was prostrate and restless. Her stomach was much swollen.' After post-mortem Dr Inman examined the body and 'was of the opinion that the woman died from inflammation of the bowels, caused or accelerated by the man kneeling upon her.' Jury returned a verdict of 'manslaughter' against Joseph Roberts, who was arrested in Court by Sergeant Leech on the coroner's warrant and conveyed to the Kingsland Road police station.

23 OCTOBER 1889

The Deptford Poisoning Case. Appearing at the Central Criminal Court, this case was famous in its day but is now all but forgotten. In May 1889 an inquest was held on the body of Sydney Bolton (11), who lived at 153 Church Street, Deptford, with Mrs

Amelia Winters and her family. He was found to have died from arsenical poisoning. It was recalled that Sydney's sister had suffered severe stomach pains during the winter of 1888/9, but she had recovered. It was also noted that elderly Mrs Amelia Winters made their meals and insured both children for £10 each. It was soon revealed she had claimed the policy and that some twelve policies for various sums were in force for 153 Church Street. Some five persons who had been insured by Mrs Winters had died since 1886. It was also noted that recent claims had been made for Elizabeth Frost (47) and William Sutton (74), who had died in similar circumstances, but the doctor had signed death certificates for natural causes. Their bodies were exhumed and both were found to contain traces of arsenical poisoning. Amelia Winters and her married daughter, Mrs Elizabeth Jane Frost (sister-in-law of the deceased Elizabeth), who, it

was suggested, helped Mrs Winter ad-minister the poison were charged with murder. *Then something strange happened.* At the indictment the divisional doctor certified that 'taking Mrs Winters into custody would endanger her life', so her daughter Elizabeth alone stood accused of the charges. On the day of the Old Bailey trial, Mr C.P. Gill, who appeared for the prosecution, stated 'the matter had been carefully considered and the course proposed to be adopted was to offer no evidence on the coroner's inquest'. The jury were directed to return a not guilty verdict.

24 OCTOBER 1877

Chief Inspector Nathaniel Druscovitch, Chief Inspector William Palmer, Inspector John Meiklejohn and Inspector George Clarke were indicted on charges of corruption at the Old Bailey. Fraudsters Harry Benson and William Kerr, captured after going on the run from a series of crimes in England and keen to reduce their sentences, had offered information on police officers in their pay, naming the four senior officers who ultimately appeared at the Old Bailey. After one of the longest trials on record, Druscovitch, Palmer and Meiklejohn were all sentenced to two years' hard labour. Superintendent Williamson spoke up for Clarke and he was acquitted. Realising he had had a narrow escape, Clarke resigned from the force.

25 OCTOBER 1877

Thomas Benjamin Pratt (27) was sentenced to death at the Central Criminal Court for the murder of Eliza Frances Brockington (35). Pratt and Brockington lived together but they were not happy. Frances was fed up with Pratt's violent behaviour towards her. He would promise to desist but the next time he took a drink or two the abuse happened all over again. Frances walked out on Pratt and sought new lodgings, but the enraged Pratt tracked her down and demanded she return. She refused so Pratt drew his knife and stabbed her to death on the corner of Wilderness Row and Goswell Road, right in front of Old Street Police Station. He walked into the police station and gave himself up. Pratt was executed at Newgate by William Marwood on 12 November 1877.

26 OCTOBER 1888

Two bare-knuckle prize-fighters in the dock. Arthur Wilkinson (21), a fish frier, and Charles Smith (20), a bootmaker, appeared at Worship Street Court for having been the principals at an illegal bare-knuckle prize-fight at the Morning Star Club, East Road, City Road, on the 19th. Inspector Capp had come to the conclusion that 'gloves were not being used because the sound of the blows was so loud'. However, the only damning evidence that stuck was a letter found on Smith in which the writer said betting was 30 to 40 on him. Wilkinson and Smith were bailed for £100 each.

Richard Mansfield.

27 OCTOBER 1888

The American actor Richard Mansfield trod the boards of Henry Irving's Lyceum Theatre in his acclaimed stage adaptation of Robert Louis Stevenson's *Dr Jekyll and Mr Hyde* (first published in 1886). Victorian sensibilities were outraged by its premise that every human being (even the respectable ones) has a demon imprisoned within them and that the right concoctions of chemicals could release it on society to gorge itself in an orgy of debauchery and malevolence. Mansfield's transformation from the upright Dr Jekyll to hideous Mr Hyde 'in all his blood curdling repulsiveness' was considered to be remarkably convincing. Due to accusations that the play was responsible in some way for the Ripper murders (on the grounds of his performance, some even suspected Mansfield himself of being the Ripper), the run of the play was cut short and terminated in its tenth week.

28 OCTOBER 1888

Following the murder investigation into the murder of Elizabeth Stride and the press speculations and fears over who the killer could be, corres-

pondence was exchanged between Police Commissioner Warren and the Home Office around this date regarding notions of a medical student being responsible. Three main suspects were initially considered. Two were traced and eliminated, but the one named as 'John Sanders' proved more elusive. Later research has revealed there were two possible candidates, the first was John William Smith Sanders, who was a medical student prone to fits of violence. He had been in Holloway asylum since February 1887. The second possible was Dr Jon William Sanders, a gynaecologist who worked at the Bethnal Green and St George's-in-the-East infirmaries. He died in 1889 aged 30.

29 OCTOBER 1888

An inquest was held at the London Hospital under the coroner, Wynne E. Baxter, on the body of Charles Jennings (42), a woodturner, a lodger at 22 Wimbold Street, Bethnal Green. His landlady, Hannah Finn, stated she had taken him home the previous Saturday, having found him asleep and much the worse for drink in a chair at the public house opposite. He went out again on the Sunday and she did not see him again 'until he was in hospital, when he told her that he had fallen from the top to the bottom of the steps at the Radical Club'. George Saunders, a member of the club, said he saw Jennings sitting on a seat, with his head bent down, in the basement of the club. He did not take any notice because he had often seen him in the same position before. George Larcher, another member, said he noticed Jennings was injured and took him to the London Hospital. House Surgeon Mr John Coulton deposed that Jennings was found to have a bad fracture of the lower leg and a bruise on his forehead; Jennings was quite drunk. Jennings died later of delirium tremens brought on by his fall. The jury agreed with the medical evidence and stated that steps ought to be taken to prohibit the sale of intoxicating liquors in clubs to persons the worse for drink.

30 OCTOBER 1888

Dr G. Danford Thomas held an inquest at the Marylebone Coroner's Court into the death of Alfred Green (46), a French polisher from High Wycombe who had died after his removal to Marylebone Workhouse, having spent thirty-eight hours in a police cell on a charge of drunkenness. It transpired that Green had been found after a fall down the stairs of Edgware Road station. Blood was flowing from a wound to his head, so he was taken to John Street Police Station for treatment. Dr Morgan treated Green and stated he was under the influence of drink. Green was charged with being drunk and incapable and placed in a cell. The following morning Green still had not recovered his senses. Dr Morgan was called and again affirmed he was recovering from the effects of drink. Kept in the cell for another night, Green was removed to the workhouse infirmary the following morning. When Green's wife came to visit him, he complained he had been 'ill-used by the police'. A witness at the inquest stated that Green appeared sober before his fall at the station; other evidence was also presented that Green was 'a sober man'. The coroner, in summing up, said that 'the divisional surgeon had committed an error of judgement in not having him removed to a proper place where he could have had the advantage of proper medical supervision'. After a long consultation, the jury returned a verdict of 'accidental death'.

31 OCTOBER

All Hallows Eve. It was not long before Jack the Ripper entered into folk legend as a popular 'bogeyman'-like monster to frighten children if they misbehaved. Many a parent was known to threaten, 'Jack the Ripper will get you!' At this time of year residents, those on business and even casual visitors to London, would often weave tall tales for fascinated young family members of how *they* saw Jack the Ripper when they were in London during the autumn of 1888. These stories have been passed down generations and there are still a few households who can tell of how Great-Aunt So-and-so or Great-Great Grandad saw Jack the Ripper flit among the shadows or run past them on the street complete with his top hat, sweeping cape, face partially obscured by an upturned collar, but the eyes, 'Oh, the eyes they burned like coals from hell itself.' In the quieter corners of the East End pubs there was many a tale told with hushed voice and narrowed eye of how the huddled figure of Polly Nichols, emitting a ghoulish green glow, had been seen lying in the gutter of Buck's Row and even how the horrible death rattle and groans of Annie Chapman had been heard on Hanbury Street. Jack the Ripper's legacy beyond the grave even extends to the skipping chant of East End children:

> Jack the Ripper's dead,
> And lying on his bed
> He cut his throat
> With Sunlight soap.
> Jack the Ripper's dead.

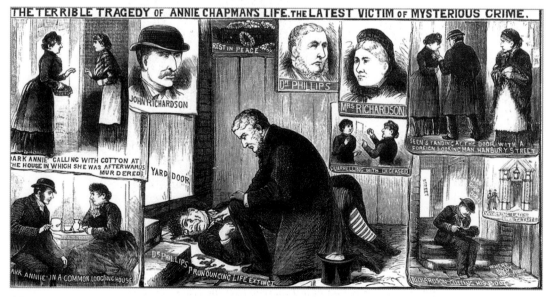

(Stewart P. Evans)

NOVEMBER

✟

A vivid portrayal of Mary Kelly, the youngest and most
attractive of all Jack the Ripper's victims, about to enter
her ragged 'rent' in Miller's Court. The atrocious injuries
inflicted on her would haunt all who saw the crime scene for
the rest of their lives.

1 NOVEMBER Tales from the Autumn of Terror

A number of clever suggestions for the apprehension of Jack the Ripper, and appliances to be worn about the neck to prevent his deadly attack, were proffered. Mr W.H. Spencer summed up this theme in a letter printed in the *Star*: '. . . a few young men of somewhat feminine appearance should be got up in disguises as females. They should wear around their necks steel collars made after the style of a ladies' collaret, coming well down the breast and likewise well down the back. My reason for this is . . . that the assassin first severs his victim's windpipe, thereby preventing her raising an alarm.'

2 NOVEMBER Criminal Types: Carriage Thieves

A common criminal type warned of in visitors' guides to London was the carriage thief. They normally operated in pairs and targeted four-wheeled cabs with their roofs laden with luggage and parcels. One thief would run behind the carriage, clamber up the back and lift off one of the parcels unbeknown to the driver and pass it to his accomplice who was running behind. The two would then run in separate directions and meet up at an agreed place later to divide the spoils. Ladies were warned to be especially careful of 'officious persons' volunteering to open or close carriage doors – in most instances they were in reality expert pickpockets!

3 NOVEMBER 1888

A report appeared in the *East London Observer* of a Sarah Tanner, 'a middle aged woman' of Rowsell Street, St Paul's Road, Mile End Old Town, being brought before the magistrates on charges of obtaining money by pretending to tell persons their fortunes at 6*d* a time. The police were notified and upon apprehension Tanner immediately recanted and swore she would never do it again. From her abode police recovered a leaf torn from *Napoleon's Book of Fate* and two packs of cards. Tanner was sent down for one month's imprisonment with hard labour.

4 NOVEMBER 1885

William Stead stands trial. Stead was one of London's most prolific journalists. He smashed on to the journalistic scene in 1885 with a series of articles about young girl prostitutes. Despite being against the law, the white slave trade was alive and well in London and Stead wanted to expose the whole sordid business. Co-opting William Booth, founder of the Salvation Army, the doyen of propriety, into his scheme to oversee no harm or abuse was involved, Stead set out to buy a virgin girl. After making contact with underworld 'fixers', the deal was done and the story published of how he had purchased a girl of 13 for five pounds. Despite exposing this hideous trade to the public, Stead was still prosecuted for what he had done and was given a three-month sentence. Booth was lucky to escape prosecution, while the fixers – the procuress and the midwife who confirmed the girl's virginity – both got six months each. Every year (until his death on the SS *Titanic* in 1912) after his imprisonment Stead wore his prison uniform on the day of his sentence in memory of his time in 'happy Holloway'.

5 NOVEMBER 1886

Reports were published of Mr Arthur Egan and his wife being found dead from bullet wounds in their bedroom at 13 Montague Street, Bloomsbury. Egan had been attended by a specialist carer for the past three years after his state of mind had prevented him working in a full-time job. Egan and his wife had taken in lodgers but most did not stay long as they were frightened away by the outbursts and strange behaviour of Egan. He mastered his condition to the degree he was able to dismiss his attendant and buy a revolver. On 4 November their maid, Lydia Chifney, found the bodies of the Egans in their bedroom. The inquest agreed with the initial opinion that Egan had shot and mortally wounded his wife before shooting himself.

6 NOVEMBER 1883

Henry Powell (24) was executed at Wandsworth. Powell had been a bricklayer employed by a Balham building firm but had been dissatisfied with his wages for the most recent job. He confronted John Briton, the son of the owner, and their disagreement developed into a fierce argument in which Powell grabbed a heavy chisel and beat Briton about the head with it. The moment of seeing red led to his arrest, trial and sentence of death. Powell was to have the unfortunate distinction of being the first criminal to be hanged by the new public executioner, Bartholomew Binns.

7 NOVEMBER Tales from the Autumn of Terror

The following letter was published in the *Daily Telegraph*:

> Sir, Can nothing be done to prevent a set of hoarse ruffians coming nightly about our suburban squares and streets yelling at the tops of their voices, and nearly frightening the life out of sensitive women and children of this neighbourhood? Last evening, for instance, their cry was 'Special' – 'Murder' – 'Paper' – 'Jack' – 'The' – 'Ripper' – 'Caught' – 'Paper' – 'Whitechapel' – 'Paper' – 'Got him at last' – Paper . . . These awful words were bawled out about nine o'clock in a quiet part of Kensington; a lady who was supping with us was so greatly distressed by these hideous bellowings that she was absolutely too unnerved to return home save in a cab because she would have to walk a hundred yards or so down a street at the end of her journey by omnibus. Now, I venture to ask sir, is it not monstrous that the police do not protect us from such flagrant and ghastly nuisances?

8 NOVEMBER Criminal Types: 'Guttersnipes'

Young lads who were so poor they were driven to lives of crime could quickly become adept at opening shop doors without ringing bells and thus pilferers of shops, stalls, railway carriages, goods wagons, pigeon lofts and fowl runs. Promising youngsters or 'guttersnipes' would often be introduced to lives of crime by older criminals. Young lads were favoured because of their agility and ability to crawl through small openings and windows to enter a property and open the door for burglar gangs. Their speed in stealing unattended wheeled vehicles was notorious. Boys as young as 9 were known to escape with horse-drawn carts!

Illustrated Police News coverage of the murder of Mary Kelly.

The remains of Mary Kelly. Photographed in situ at 13 Miller's Court, this is one of the earliest and most horrific crime scene photographs of all time. (*Stewart P. Evans*)

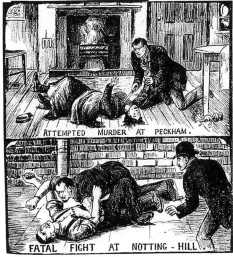

Another lurid cover of the *Illustrated Police News* carries graphic depictions based on the account given by George Hutchinson. His description is just one of many, most of which seemed to cancel each other out. The lack of a clear description was even mocked in one of the letters purportedly from the killer and recalled by Melville Macnaghten in *Days of my Years*:

> I'm not a butcher, I'm not a Yid,
> Nor yet a foreign skipper,
> But I'm your own light-hearted friend,
> Yours truly, Jack the Ripper.

9 November 1888

The alleged final victim of Jack the Ripper. Mary Jane (or Jeanette) Kelly was remembered as a striking figure in the East End. Known on the streets as 'Black Mary', she was younger than most of the prostitutes. She was 25, blue-eyed and tall with a fine head of hair reaching almost to her waist. Her pitch in front of the Ten Bells on Commercial Street was well known and woe betide any other unfortunate who trod on it, for she had brawled and won, 'pulling hair out by fistfuls', on a number of occasions. On the night of her murder Mary was seen with a short, stout man with a carroty moustache by fellow lodger Mrs Cox. Kelly was later heard singing 'Only a Violet I Plucked from My Mother's Grave when a Boy'. The last witness to see her alive was an old acquaintance named George Hutchinson. He had spoken to her at about 2 a.m. and seen her go off with another man carrying a small parcel in his left hand with 'a kind of a strap round it'. He had heard them laugh and her say 'All right' to him, and the man said, 'You will be all right for what I have told you.' He then placed his right hand around her shoulders. At about 3.30 or 4 a.m. two neighbours heard a cry of 'Oh! Murder,' but they were not sure where it came from. Mary lived just off Dorset Street in one of 'McCarthy's Rents' at 13 Miller's Court. She was facing eviction for non-payment of rent. On the morning of the 9th McCarthy sent his assistant, Thomas Bowyer, to collect the debt. He received no reply and pushed his hand through a broken pane of the window and moved the flimsy curtain to one side to see if she was in. The walls were splashed up like an abattoir and on the blood-soaked mattress was what had once been Mary Kelly and was now the final most horrifically mutilated victim of Jack the Ripper. Inspector Walter Beck was summoned from Commercial Street and was soon joined at the scene by Inspector Abberline, George Bagster Phillips, the H Division Surgeon and even young PC Walter Dew (the man who would later become world famous as the man who arrested Crippen). None of them ever forgot what they saw at Miller's Court.

Poignantly, the resignation of Sir Charles Warren (tendered on 8 November), the man many held responsible for the failure of the police to capture Jack the Ripper, was accepted and ann-ounced on this day.

10 November 1888

Queen Victoria sent a telegram to the Marquis of Salisbury, the prime minister, from Balmoral expressing her concern and suggestions for actions to apprehend Jack the Ripper: 'This new most ghastly murder shows the absolute necessity for some very decided action. All courts must be lit, & our detectives improved. They are not what they should be . . .'

Queen Victoria.

11 November 1888

A man with his face blackened and wearing spectacles startled a woman named Humphreys outside George Yard, Whitechapel. She challenged him but he simply laughed and ran off. Humphreys screamed 'Murder!' and a crowd was soon in pursuit of the strange man. Luckily the police got to him first before the mob and took him into custody. He turned out to be Dr William Holt, a doctor attached to St George's Hospital, and keen amateur detective, who was attempting to track the Ripper using various disguises. He was released the next day.

IS DETECTION A FAILURE ?

In the interests of the Gutter Gazette and of the Criminal Classes, the Sensational Interviewer dogs the Detective's footsteps, and throws the strong light of publicity on his work. Under these circumstances, it is not surprising that Detection should prove a failure.

Illustration from *Punch*, 1888.

12 November 1888

An inquest was held at Guy's Hospital into the death of Elizabeth Billett (31) of 91 Boyson Road, Walworth. Mr and Mrs Billett had returned from a night out with Mr Billett very drunk, and they were heard talking loudly in the kitchen. The sound of a lamp exploding followed and Elizabeth's sister, who also lived in the house, came rushing downstairs and discovered that Elizabeth's black cashmere dress had caught fire and she was trying to put it out. The sister ran into the street to call for help and a carman named Harris came to the rescue, extinguished the flames and took Mrs Billett to hospital. She said, 'My husband knocked the table over and broke the lamp and set me on fire.' Poor Mrs Billett died of her extensive burns a few days later. The inquest verdict was 'accidental death'.

Police lines turn the crowd in Trafalgar Square, Bloody Sunday, 13 November 1887.

13 NOVEMBER 1887

Bloody Sunday. Unemployment and poverty had grown to such proportions in London that jobless agitators started camping in Trafalgar Square in an attempt to draw attention to their plight. Political meetings began to be held in the square with increasing regularity, with the speeches becoming more and more inciteful and impassioned. Sir Charles Warren saw the warning signs and pressured Home Secretary Matthews to declare such meetings in and around the square illegal. A meeting that challenged this prohibition was called for at 2.30 p.m. on this day. Warren personally took 2,000 of his men to Trafalgar Square to meet this challenge. He also had two squadrons of Life Guards on standby at Horse Guards Parade with two magistrates to read the Riot Act if necessary. At 3.45 an unruly mob armed with sticks, iron bars, knives, stones and bricks approached the square intent on storming it. The police held firm, but, concerned about the escalating violence, Warren ordered the Life Guards in at 4.05. In all, 4,000 constables, 300 mounted police, 300 Grenadier Guards and 300 Life Guards were deployed to quell the riot. Over 150 of the crowd were treated for injuries and over 300 were arrested. Most were dismissed with warnings or fines but some got imprisonment with hard labour varying between one and six months.

14 NOVEMBER 1899

Thomas Skeffington (20) spent his last night in the condemned cell of Newgate Prison, knowing he would keep his appointment with James Billington at nine o'clock the following morning. Skeffington, an unemployed barman, had been seen to leave the Tyssen Arms on Dalston Lane with a married woman named Florrie Wells (27). He put his arm around her neck in what appeared to be a friendly manner and then walked away, leaving the woman to stumble and fall, calling out, 'He stabbed me.' A boy named James Arnold stated at the inquest that he saw Skeffington strike her twice in the throat. A brave man named Richard Masters caught Skeffington up in Holly Street and challenged him as to what he had done. Skeffington replied, ' I did it with this' and produced a large clasp knife, adding, 'I am going to the station.' As he appeared to be going the wrong way, Masters escorted him to the police. He was tried and found guilty of murder and received the full extent of the law.

Police and rioters clash on 'Bloody Sunday', 13 November 1887.

15 November 1892

Thomas Neill Cream was executed at Newgate for the murder of Matilda Clover. Born in Glasgow in 1850, Cream qualified in medicine in Canada and practised in Britain, America and Canada – probably to avoid capture for his habitual illegal medical practices, such as abortion. When he returned to Britain in October 1891, he had just been released after serving ten years of a 'life' sentence in Joliet Penitentiary. Only a few days after his arrival back in England he was up to his old tricks. A poor 'unfortunate' named Ellen Donworth (19) collapsed in the Waterloo Road and died in agony before she reached hospital. She managed to say she had been given a drink with 'white stuff' in it by a man she had met at the Waterloo Hotel who matched Cream's description. A few days later, just hours after entertaining Cream at her residence, Matilda Clover was seized by agonising stomach pains and died at 8.30 a.m. Her servant, Lucy Rose, got a good look at Cream and gave an excellent description of him to the police. Cream disappeared back to the United States again for another six months but he was back in 1892 and had a 'double event' in which he managed to get both Emma Shrivell (18) and her lodging-house companion Alice Marsh to sample his deadly wares. One died on the way to St Thomas's Hospital, the other a short while after arrival. Cream was a sad little self-publicist and produced posters and letters making accusations, and appeared to want to increase his 'importance' by demonstrating his knowledge of the crimes. He was soon apprehended. He had opened his mouth once too often and even one of the prostitutes to whom he had given tablets,

Thomas Neill Cream.

but who had palmed them off because 'she didn't like the look of them', came forward. Found guilty and sentenced to death, this pathetic little man went to the gallows on this day and died with a deluded lie on his lips. According to executioner Billington, just after the hood and noose had been adjusted and as he pushed the lever, Cream piped up, 'I'm Jack the . . .'. The fall of the trap silenced him for ever.

16 November 1898

The newspapers recorded the execution at Newgate of John Ryan (30). A bricklayer's labourer, Ryan suffered the ultimate penalty for the murder of PC James Baldwin by stabbing in Wilmer Gardens on the Kingsland Road. Executioner James Billington gave Ryan a drop of 7ft 6in, and the medical officer, Dr Scott, declared death was instantaneous.

17 November 1888

A Swedish man named Nikaner Benelius was arrested by PC Imhoff for burglary at the home of Harriet Rowe on Buxton Street, Mile End. In a move fuelled by xenophobia, fear and desperation to find Jack the Ripper, Benelius was detained on suspicion of being the murderer, but it was soon clear that he was totally innocent of the murders and he was cleared of all charges.

18 November 1881

The police remained baffled after German baker Urban Napoleon Stanger disappeared after leaving his bakery on Lever Street, St Luke's, in a state of disarray on 13 November. Dark rumours spread about murder and secret disposal of the body, and no corpse was ever found. Another German baker named Stumm was arrested for forging Stanger's name to some securities. At his trial Stanger's wife gave strong evidence against Stumm, but the jury were not convinced he could be convicted of murder. Stumm was given the stiffest sentence for his other misdemeanours and was sent down for ten years.

19 November 1897

Fire broke out on the first floor of a warehouse on Hamsell Street, in the City. Soon a crowd gathered to watch the blaze. Most people assumed the fire brigade had been summoned, but this was not so. By the time the first steamer fire engine had arrived, the fire had taken firm hold and spread to the adjoining buildings. Fanned by high winds it spread yet further to Jewin Street, Jewin Crescent and the back of Well Street. It took no less than 60 fire appliances, and 300 firemen and an estimated 15 million gallons of water to get the blaze under control. The fire left the majority of Hamsell Street 'nothing else than a heterogeneous pile of masonry, twisted ironwork and burnt goods'. A total of over 100 warehouses covering 100,000 square yards were totally destroyed. At the City of London inquiry it was decided that the fire had actually been caused by an arsonist.

20 NOVEMBER 1888

A suspected 'Ripper' attack took place: Annie Farmer had her neck gashed in Satchell's common lodging house at 19 George Street, Spitalfields. She had arrived at the house about seven o'clock in the morning with a man, and both were the worse for drink. At nine o'clock, screams came from Farmer's room. Some men in the kitchen rushed upstairs, meeting Annie coming down the stairs nursing a severe gash to her throat. All she said was, 'He's done it,' pointing outside on to the street. A man had been noticed leaving the building but he was never traced. Dr George Bagster Phillips stitched up the wound and had her removed to Commercial Street Police Station, away from the growing crowd in the street.

21 NOVEMBER Prisons and Punishments: Pentonville Prison

This prison on Caledonian Road, Islington, was opened in 1842, and was built to American designs but still maintaining the 'separate system'. It was originally intended as a processing prison for convicts due for transportation. If a prisoner here behaved they might earn a ticket of leave that would allow them the freedom to seek employment in the New World. If prisoners did not toe the line at Pentonville, they could end up working on a chain gang in all weathers. When transportation ended and the prison commissioners took control in 1877, Pentonville became the shorter sentence prison for petty offenders in the London area, a role it serves for about 800 inmates to this day.

22 NOVEMBER 1891

London was enveloped in a dense yellow fog from Christmas time until the New Year. 'Russian' influenza (so named after its first appearance in Bokhara, Russia in May 1889) spread to England via St Petersburg. It grew to epidemic proportions and clogged the wards of the capital's hospitals, especially the London Hospital, who admitted hundreds from Whitechapel. Because of the terrible conditions in which many from the East End existed, they had the least chance of survival and hundreds succumbed to this virulent strain of broncho-pneumonia. It has been suggested that it was from this epidemic Prince Edward, (Eddy) the Duke of Clarence caught his illness and died after being moved away to Sandringham, the country retreat of the royal family in Norfolk.

Exercising in the yard at Pentonville, *c.* 1878. Prisoners were kept in the 'separate and silent' system: they wore masks so they could only see the floor beneath them and had to maintain the length of chain distance from other inmates so they could not communicate with each other in any way.

23 November 1888

Thomas Hurley (19) appeared at Thames Police Court charged on remand with assaulting PC Wilcock 148H while in the execution of his duty. Wilcock had been standing outside a pub on Fieldgate Street, Whitechapel, when Hurley came up and tripped him into the road. This act drew a mocking crowd and some 'put the boot in' while he was on the ground. Wilcock got up and arrested Hurley, who called the crowd to 'rescue me'. The crowd moved in on the officer and, before he knew what was happening, he had been stabbed on the right shoulder blade. Hurley denied stabbing the constable and was committed for trial.

24 November 1888

Dr Francis Tumblety ran out on his bail (having been arrested for an act of gross indecency with other men on 7 November), fled to America and assumed the name Frank Townsend. Tumblety was an Irish-American quack doctor and braggart known to have a hatred of women. He was pursued to the United States by Inspector Andrews, but he failed to locate him. Tumblety was later named by Chief Inspector John Littlechild (in a personal letter to George R. Sims discovered by author Stewart P. Evans in 1993) as the chief suspect for the crimes of Jack the Ripper – and he

Pamphlet produced by Francis Tumblety at the time he was accused of collusion in the assassination of President Lincoln. (*Stewart P. Evans*)

had slipped through the fingers of the police! He was a convincing suspect who fits the modern 'profile' of a serial killer. Such killers often take trophies. For instance, Annie Chapman was known to wear two brass rings, which were missing when her body was found in the backyard of 29 Hanbury Street. When Tumblety finally died of a heart condition at St John's Hospital, St Louis, in 1903, among his few effects were 'two imitation rings worth $3'.

25 NOVEMBER 1888

A Continental gentleman residing at Bacon's Hotel in Fitzroy Square was questioned by the police after a prostitute named Annie Cook became suspicious of him. Cook was offered a sovereign for intercourse and five more to spend the night with him. The size of the offer made her doubt his motives and she informed the police. The man, who gave his name as Alfred Parent, proved he was from Paris and provided alibis which proved he was not involved in the Whitechapel murders.

26 NOVEMBER 1887

Death at the Bank of England. An inquest was held at the Bank of England before Mr Langham the City Coroner into the death of Charles Rose (52), comptroller of the stock department. After eating a large breakfast, Mr Rose had been late and had to run to catch his train. When he arrived at work he complained of stomach pains and vomited a great deal. Medicine was procured from a neighbouring chemist's shop that the deceased drank and said he felt better, but subsequently he was found lying dead on the floor of his private room in the stock department. Mr Pendick, the surgeon who had conducted the post-mortem, pronounced that 'death was due to a syncope brought on by the deceased eating a hearty meal and then hurrying to catch his train'. A verdict in accordance with the surgeon's findings was recorded.

27 NOVEMBER Criminal Types: Letter-Box Thieves or 'Fishers'

The letter-box thief was to be found in the more affluent areas of London where people might send money, valuables or indiscreet letters (ideal for selling on to blackmailers). By noting the times a certain street pillar box was emptied by the postman, the thief was able to judge when the box was likely to be full. When the coast was clear, the thief would 'fish' for letters by means of a line with a lead weight attached to the end which was smeared with bird lime. The lime stuck to the letters and allowed them to be pulled out.

28 NOVEMBER Tales from the Autumn of Terror

Much thought was expressed in the press about what precautions could be taken by the ladies of Whitechapel. One scheme dubbed 'belling the cats' suggested the girls carry police whistles and be instructed in a signalling system. Hardly practical, the idea of carrying a police whistle did appeal as a safety measure to a few of the girls. One woman named Eleanor Candey was picked up by a man on the Whitechapel Road. As they proceeded to less public surroundings, she confided in the man that she didn't go out at night without her whistle since the Ripper murders, to which the man, who was

The Thames Police Station noticeboard.

drunk, replied, 'And I never go out without my trusty little knife. . . . If you want to know who I am – I am the Whitechapel Murderer!' Candey immediately drew her whistle and blasted on it with every drop of breath she had. the man ran off and collided with a police officer before a mob was roused. Arrested for indecent assault the man turned out to be a licensed victualler named Joseph Woods – he had alibis for the murders, and had only said he was the Ripper out of ill-thought bravado!

29 NOVEMBER Criminal Types: 'Snuffer Gangs'

In the lowest pubs of the East End, especially those nearest the docks and along the Ratcliff Highway (re-Christened St George's Street by 1888 because of its infamous reputation), were the haunts of the 'Snuffer Gangs'. Newly paid-off seamen would stride into pubs to be heartily greeted by groups of men 'fascinated' to learn of the seafaring life and insistent on buying the seaman a drink. Some brown powder was added surreptitiously to the foaming draught by one of his new-found companions. If the unsuspecting matelot downed the draught, he was soon sleepy and stupefied and was hustled from the bar by his friends 'to get some air'. He was then bundled down some dark alley or isolated river steps, pinioned, severely beaten and robbed of all he had. If after this 'doing over' he still looked like being able to raise the alarm, the gangs would throw their victim headlong into the river from whence his body was recovered a few days later.

30 NOVEMBER 1887

The inquest was held at University College Hospital into the death of George Michael Graham, a stockbroker, of 47 Woburn Place, Russell Square. Graham had met up with his friend Daniel Francis Doherty, an American stockbroker, to go to Doherty's house for dinner. They drove there in a cab discussing the £600 of borrowed money Doherty had lost. Doherty said he thought he should not pay it back but Graham stated he thought he should. At Woburn Place, Doherty went into the bedroom and Graham casually sat down and read the newspaper, while Mrs Doherty was overseeing dinner. Doherty then came out of the bedroom and shot Graham. At the inquest Mrs Doherty claimed her husband had simply been going to show Graham his new pistol. Graham received fast medical attention and was able to give a statement to Inspector Pinhorn of E Division. The bullet had passed through the abdomen, causing rupture of the intestines and Graham died of the resultant peritonitis. Appearing at the Old Bailey on 20 December, Doherty was found guilty of manslaughter with wilful violence and was sentenced to twenty years' penal servitude.

DECEMBER

Detonation of a Fenian bomb on one of the piers of
London Bridge, 13 December 1884. City workers
returning home were knocked off their feet and horses
bolted but incredibly nobody was seriously hurt.

1 December 1887

Dr (later Sir) Arthur Conan Doyle's first Sherlock Holmes story 'A Study in Scarlet' was published in *Beeton's Christmas Annual*. He was paid £25 for his trouble. Doyle went on to write fifty-six Sherlock Holmes short stories and four novellas, which were mostly published as part works in the *Strand Magazine*. Doyle grew to hate the master detective he had created. He wanted to write more on other subjects and explore spiritualism but the public demanded more Holmes stories. Despite giving his master detective twenty-seven murder cases, numerous threats to his life in various forms, a morphine habit and sending him to his 'death' on the Reichenbach Falls with his arch enemy Professor Moriarty, Sherlock Holmes returned and remains one of the most read and recognisable characters of detective fiction.

2 December Criminal Types: The Female Pickpocket

Often respectably attired to avoid suspicion, the female pickpocket was far more sophisticated than the common street 'dipper'. Her kind were far more wily! False arms and hands masked by gloves and muffs left her real hands free inside her clothes to dip out from side panels to pick the pockets of those sat beside her on omnibuses and tramcars. Hidden pockets in their voluminous skirts received the takings.

3 December Prisons and Punishments: The Crank

The crank was a widely adopted means of occupying prisoners within the 'separate system' in British prisons during the latter half of the nineteenth century. In certain London prisons like Wandsworth they were widely used instead of the treadwheel, while in most prisons they were used to occupy refractory prisoners in their solitary cells. Operated by a single prisoner, the crank comprised a drum on a metal pillar or a handle set into a wall with a dial to register the number of times the crank handle had been turned – usually about twenty times a minute, a typical target being a total of 10,000 revolutions in eight and a half hours. If the target was not achieved in time, the prisoner was given no food until the dial registered the required total. A legacy of the crank remains in our language today. If the prisoner found this task too easy or proved refractory, the prison warder would come and tighten the screw, making the handle harder to turn. Hence the prison parlance for prison warder has, for generations, been 'the screw'.

An inmate on one of the cranks in Pentonville Prison.

4 DECEMBER Tales from the Autumn of Terror

Alongside the Whitechapel Vigilance Committee operated a number of other groups and individuals who attempted to ward off and apprehend Jack the Ripper. Among the most notable of these groups were the street patrols from Toynbee Hall, who walked the back streets, courtyards and alleyways of Spitalfields during the hours of darkness. Toynbee Hallers were all graduates of Oxford or Cambridge Universities doing settlement work (an early type of social work) in the East End under the watchful eye of their founder warden, Canon Samuel Barnett. After months of treading where many were afeared to go after dark, through stench-filled, decaying houses and dingy streets and being exposed to almost every human degradation, the long hours caught up with the brave young men and they finally gave up their patrol work in February 1889.

Toynbee Hall vigilance patrol, *Illustrated London News*.

5 DECEMBER 1887

The fatal casualty of Bloody Sunday. It was incredible that no one was killed outright on Bloody Sunday (see 13 November, p. 170). Over 150 were treated for injuries and the hospitals were filled with serious cases for weeks afterwards. On this day an inquest was conducted at St Martin's Vestry Hall, Charing Cross, into the circumstances of the death of Alfred Linnell (41), a law writer of Took's Court, Cursitor Street, who died from injuries received in Northumberland Avenue during the 'Bloody Sunday' riots. Slipping, he fell down and was 'trampled by a mounted policeman and several others while they were clearing the streets'. Rushed to Charing Cross Hospital, he was operated on for a compound fracture of the thigh. All appearances suggested full recovery but blood poisoning set in and it killed him. Accidental death was recorded.

6 December 1888

Joseph Isaacs (30), a Polish Jew, was arrested near Drury Lane and taken to Bow Street Police Station. What he was charged with was not immediately apparent and the rumour mill (no doubt fuelled by xenophobia and paranoia) soon assumed Isaacs was arrested on suspicion of being Jack the Ripper. He had in fact been arrested for the theft of a 30s watch. His alibi for the Ripper crimes was truly impeccable – he was under police obsevation for another crime at time! On this same day Aaron Davis Cohen was arrested in the course of a police raid on a brothel. When he appeared the following day at the Thames Police Court, Cohen was described as a lunatic found wandering at large. He was removed on 21 December to Colney Hatch Asylum, where he was admitted under the name of David Cohen. A violent and disruptive patient, he died of

pulmonary tuberculosis on 20 October 1889. Ripperologist Martin Fido, who has researched the institution archives of the period, is convinced Cohen is the man elusively referred to by Metropolitan Police Assistant Commissioner Dr Robert Anderson (appointed 31 August 1888) in his *The Lighter Side of My Official Life* (1910) as 'the individual who we suspected (who) was caged in an asylum'. In his personal copy of the book, Chief Inspector Donald Swanson, the man who was in overall charge of the Ripper investigation from September 1888 as desk officer in charge, reporting to Anderson) annotated the name 'Kosminski' beside Anderson's allusion to 'the individual who we suspected'. The trouble is that Swanson also went on to note that Kosminski died soon after his incarceration in Colney Hatch (see 15 July, p. 106)!

7 December 1885

Daniel Minahan (28), a labourer, was executed at Newgate for the murder of his wife, Bridget. Minahan had overslept and placed the blame squarely on his wife for not waking him sufficiently early. Outraged by the quarrel, he took up a hammer and bludgeoned her to death. Minahan gave himself up to the police, stood trial, was found guilty and sentenced to death. Concern was shown at the prison after the recent incident at an execution at Norwich Gaol (15 September 1885) where Robert Goodale, the Walsoken murderer, had had his head torn off when the rope 'bit' after he was dropped through the trap. A drop shorter than than prescribed by the Home Office was ordered by local judiciary to be limited to 5ft 3in. His death was recorded as instantaneous, the jury of the coroner's court making especial note that the executed man's face 'bore a perfectly placid expression without the slightest trace of pain'.

8 December 1889

News spread of the murderous attack on William Hall by William James (33). Hall was walking home along Marshalsea Street, Borough, with workmate George Figes from their jobs at the GPO sorting office on the night of 7 December when a woman 'who had been in the company of a man' came up to them crying she had been 'grossly insulted' by the man. He had asked her if she knew in whose company she was and said he was Jack the Ripper. Out of the shadows came William James (who described himself as a hawker but was probably a pimp) and hit the man who had been with the tearful woman. The man stumbled away towards Borough with a crowd in pursuit. Hall and his workmate crossed the road to watch the crowd run off. Suddenly Hall received a heavy blow to the side of his head from James, knocking him to the pavement with a sickening thud. James ran off but was picked up later by a PC Freeman 327M. When James was questioned he claimed *he* was 'Jack the Ripper' and was taken to Stone's End Police Station. Hall was also assisted to the station where he identified James as his attacker. Hall was then removed to Guy's Hospital by police ambulance where he died a few hours later from his fractured skull and a blood clot on the brain. At the inquest the jury returned a verdict of wilful murder against William James and he was detained for trial at the Old Bailey.

9 December 1872

Augustus Elliott (25) was executed at Newgate for the murder of Mary Jane Aldington (22), who lodged with her friend Miss King in Northport Street, Hoxton. Elliott and Aldington had visited music halls, pubs and places of entertainment together for three or four years. Mary Jane returned to her room with Elliott on 14 September and he stayed the following night too. The following day the landlady heard three pistol shots from their room. Alarmed by this she gathered some of her neighbours and forced the door, which was locked on the inside. The couple were both wounded and the room showed signs of a struggle. The girl had received two gunshots to the head and face while Elliott was bleeding from a wound to his head. A revolver was discovered in the room. Elliott and Aldington were removed to St Bartholomew's Hospital where the bullets were removed, and both appeared to make good progress. Tragically, Mary Jane developed complications and died, whereas Elliott went on to make a good recovery. He said they had rowed, she had thrown the ring he had given her back at him and the situation had ended with the shooting. Elliott said he wished he had 'finished it'.

10 December 1876

Charles O'Donnell spent his last full day in the condemned cell at Newgate for the murder of his wife in a fit of rage after numerous arguments. O'Donnell had an irreproachable past. He had served twenty-two years in the army and received a military pension, and had until recently been in charge of a ward in the cholera hospital. His life changed after meeting the woman who would become his wife.

O'Donnell married after a whirlwind romance of six months but the union did not to prove a happy one. Once sentence was passed O'Donnell acknowledged the justness of his sentence, he was a model prisoner in every way. He was despatched at 8a.m. sharp on 11 December and buried within four hours of execution. As per the usual practice, within the prison walls, his body was covered in quicklime and his grave marked with a stone only bearing his initials.

11 December 1878

Mrs Rachel Samuel, a widow of over 70, was found murdered and lying in a pool of blood in her home in Burton Crescent, Euston Road. She had been beaten round the head with a hat rack. Her servant, Mary Donovan (40), did not return that night and was swiftly arrested. Her clothes were stained and human blood was found on the soles of her boots. Mr Flowers, the Bow Street magistrate, did not deem this sufficient evidence for trial. Donovan was released and the murder remained officially 'unsolved'.

12 December 1888

An inquest was held at the George and Dragon on St George's Road, Camberwell, on the death of an infant child, Nellie, while in the care of Mrs Sarah Sinclair. It was stated Mrs Sinclair, who was registered under the Infant Life Protection Act to have the custody of young children at 50 Maxted Road, East Dulwich, had advertised about three weeks previously for another child. She received a reply from Ellen Gardiner, a domestic servant, with regard to her infant daughter, Nellie. Mrs Sinclair went to visit the mother and father of the child, and when she arrived she found the child 'lying on the floor. It had no clothes on and was carried to Mrs Sinclair's home on the 25th October in an old Ulster.' Mrs Sinclair received small sums of money at various times but the child became ill with thrush and eventually died. The poor little infant had been attended at the last by the parish doctor, but there was clear evidence of neglect. Dr Sergeant pointed out death was due to 'inanition through the want of proper nourishment'. The jury returned a verdict in accordance with the medical evidence but pointed out they considered a doctor should have been obtained earlier.

13 December 1880

William Herbert (54) and George Pavey (29) were executed at Newgate for two separate crimes of murder. Herbert had shot his sister-in-law, a Mrs Messenger, in Finsbury Park and afterwards unsuccessfully attempted to commit suicide. Despite a plea of insanity, the death sentence was not commuted. Pavey's crime was 'atrocious'. He had violated and murdered a little girl, the child of his master, who had placed her in his care for the day. Both men stood on the scaffold, side by side, and were sent to eternity by executioner Marwood.

14 December 1897

One of the leading actors of his day, William Terriss was stabbed to death at his private entrance to the Adelphi Theatre by Richard A. Prince. Prince, known to acquaintances as 'Mad Archie', was an inveterate letter writer who sent high-handed missives to theatrical managers who offended him or sent fawning letters of commiseration or congratulations to royalty or celebrities depending on the occasion. He was thought harmless by most. Terriss tolerated him and granted the frustrated actor more than one audience but finally refused to see him any more. On the 13th, Prince attempted to get a complimentary ticket to the vaudeville theatre which adjoined the Adelphi. He was turned down, made a scene, stormed out and went home to brood. His jealousy centred on Terriss, and the foll-owing day he enacted his twisted revenge. Convicted of the murder but found insane, he spent the rest of his years at Broadmoor Criminal Lunatic Asylum, occa-sionally putting on concerts with the other inmates.

William Terriss.

15 December 1894

Police were frustrated by their lack of progress in investi-gating the murder of Mr Martin, a night watchman at the Café Royal for fifteen years. He was found by the arriving morning staff on 6 December shot through the head and had been dead some hours. He was discovered in the place he always stationed himself, on a plush-covered settee near the Glasshouse Street entrance, where he was surrounded with mirrors and could command a view of the length and breadth of the building. Barmaids and others sleeping above the crime scene heard nothing. His murder was never solved.

16 December 1888

The noted coachman James William Selby (1843–88) died of exposure. His exploits and speed in piloting his coach 'Old Times' were renowned. In the year of his death Selby won a bet for covering the 108-mile journey from London to Brighton in seven hours and fifty minutes. His demise did not surprise those who knew him well. Rain, wind and snow would not deter this brave coachman, but there were only so many times he could get so cold that his hat froze to his head and had to be steamed off!

17 December 1883

Patrick O'Donnell (28) was executed at Newgate for the murder of James Casey. An Irish faction known as the 'Invincibles' had murdered Thomas Henry Burke (Permanent Under-Secretary for Ireland) and Lord Frederick Cavendish (Chief Secretary of State for Ireland) in May 1882. In what became known as the Phoenix Park Murders in Dublin, twenty-seven conspirators were tracked down by police. Three turned informer, one of whom was James Carey – who had been leader of the gang! He was the star witness for the prosecution in exchange for his life. Ultimately five of their number were sent to the gallows for the crime. Carey was given passage to South Africa for his own safety, but while being transported from Cape Town to Port Elizabeth on board the SS *Melrose*, Carey was shot by Patrick O'Donnell, an Irish nationalist. He was found guilty, sentenced to death and executed.

18 December 1876

Silas Barlow was executed for the murder of Ellen Sloper at Horsemonger Lane Gaol.

Patrick O'Donnell in the dock.

19 December 1888

A body was recovered from Surrey Canal at Camberwell. Dr Ernest Berkley was called to examine the corpse and reported that it was that 'of a man unknown, aged about 30, who was found with his throat cut and legs tied together with stout leather bootlaces just below the knees'. The inquest was held at George and Dragon, St George's Road, Camberwell. The only clues to his identity were his clothes, which appeared to be those of a coal porter, the letters 'C.H.' tattooed on his left arm, a shamrock on the right and a tattooed ring on one of his fingers. The inquest concluded, 'how he received his injuries and got into the water there was no evidence to show'.

20 December 1888

The murdered body of prostitute Rose Mylett (26) (a.k.a. Lizzie Davies) was found by Police Sergeant Golding and a constable in Clarke's Yard off High Street, Poplar. The initial word on the street was that Jack the Ripper had struck again, but in this case there was almost no sign of struggle or violence and 'the face was perfectly placid'. She had been strangled with 'a four lag cord'. It was asked at the inquest if this was possibly the method that Jack used to stop his victims crying out, and that on this occasion he had been disturbed so he could not inflict his usual hideous trademarks. It was clearly pointed out by Dr Phillips, who had examined the Ripper victims and Mylett, that none of the Ripper victims showed any evidence of strangulation. The only thing Rose Mylett's murderer really had in common with Jack the Ripper was that neither of them was ever brought to justice.

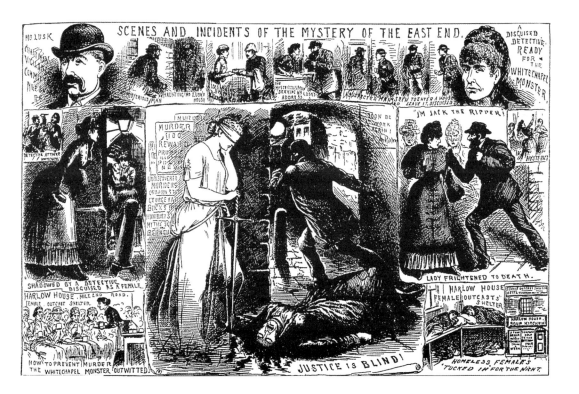

21 December 1888

The findings were published of the inquest held at Red House Coffee Palace, High Street, Tottenham, into the death of James Eli Hawkins (53), the stationmaster at Tottenham Hale station. Obnery Alldis of White Cottage, Tottenham, a porter, stated that he was on the station at 8.30 a.m. on the previous Tuesday morning when Hawkins had come up to him, remarked about some trucks on the siding and set off across the tracks to give instruction about them. It was a foggy morning and Alldis soon lost sight of his station master. Gerald Fitzgerald, the station signalman, deposed that the lines were clear and he had 'signals off' for the two trains that passed through the station within a few minutes of 8.30. Alfred Underill was the engine driver of the 1.30 a.m. train from Whitcombe, which passed through the station at 8.32, and 'as he was leaving the station he felt the engine jump as if he had run over something'. On reaching the next signal box, he stopped the train to report the incident. It was so foggy neither signalman nor driver could see ten yards in front of them. Alldis crossed the metals a short while later and found the body of Hawkins lying in the four-foot way. He said, 'His body was cut to pieces and a shutter had to be procured before the remains could be removed.' The jury returned a verdict of accidental death with a warning for the railway company that it should take greater precautions for the safety of their employees during such dense fogs.

22 December 1888

Theophil Hanhart (24), lately a French and German master at a school near Bath, appeared at Dalston Police Court. He was said to resemble the description of Jack the Ripper. While standing, gazing fixedly at the waters from the bank of Regent's Canal at Haggerston, he confessed to a passing police constable that he was 'the cause of the Whitechapel murders, and he was very uneasy in his mind about it'. The medical examiner stated that Hanhart was suffering from mental derangement and was 'not fit to be at large'. Inspector Reid from Whitechapel said he was satisfied the prisoner could not have committed the murders. Hanhart was removed by cab to Shoreditch Infirmary.

23 December 1890

The execution took place of Mrs Mary Eleanor Wheeler (24), known to infamy by her alias of Mrs Pearcey, for the murder of Phoebe Hogg and her baby daughter. Mary Wheeler had assumed the name of Pearcey from a carpenter with whom she had lived but never married. For the past two years she had resided at 2 Priory Street, Kentish Town, and had among her love interests a local furniture remover named Frank Hogg. Hogg had an affair with young Phoebe Hogg and got her pregnant. He married Phoebe but carried on seeing Mrs Pearcey, and in fact he employed Pearcey in the marital home to nurse Mrs Hogg and the baby! On Friday 24 October 1890 Mrs Pearcey invited Mrs Hogg and baby Phoebe around for tea. At seven o'clock the same evening Mrs Hogg's body was discovered on a building site in Crossfield Street. Her throat had been cut and her body mutilated to such a degree that word went out that Jack the Ripper was up to his old tricks again. On Sunday the 26th the body of baby Phoebe was found on waste ground near the Finchley Road. Frank Hogg had not been too perturbed by the absence of his wife, because he thought she had probably gone to visit her sick father. When he saw the newspaper reports about the body, his concerns were raised, so he sent his sister Clara round to Mrs Pearcey and the two ladies went to the mortuary to view the body. Clara recognised her sister but Mrs Pearcey insisted it was not. This strange behaviour caused the police to visit Pearcey. Bloodstains were found on a kitchen knife and poker as well as on her kitchen floor, and when asked about this she spoke vaguely about 'killing mice'. Hogg was jeered and hissed at the inquest and funeral of his wife and child. Pearcey stood trial, was found guilty and was hanged on this day by executioner Berry at Newgate. The traditional execution bell that had tolled at St Sepulchre's Church on the occasions of executions for hundreds of years did not ring on this day and the tradition was discontinued.

24 December 1888

Dr Roslyn D'Onston Stephenson (real name Robert Donston Stephenson) persuaded his acquaintance, George Marsh, to go to the police and give a statement to the effect that Dr Morgan Davies of the London Hospital was Jack the Ripper. Stephenson also sent a number of letters to the police directly accusing Davies of the murders. Obsessed with the idea that the Ripper sodomised his victims and that Dr Davies had demonstated this method *too* well in one of his lectures, Stephenson was convinced he was the murderer. Stephenson was a known occultist, drinker and hallucinogenic drug taker. In later years he became a Ripper suspect in his own right; Baroness Vittoria Cremers even told journalists in the 1920s that she found ties encrusted in blood hidden in Stephenson's room.

Dr Roslyn D'Onston Stephenson. *(Stewart P. Evans)*

25 December 1888

Esther Reynolds was walking out on Whitechapel High Street in her Christmas holidays when her silver chain and locket were snatched from her neck by two young men. Two boys named Watson and Huer were standing in Angel Alley and had been aware of the men, who they knew to be Henry Yatton (19) and James Davis (18), watching Miss Reynolds. Davis said to the boys, 'Stand out of the way and give him room to run.' They then saw Yatton go up to the girl, snatch the chain and run down the alley with Davis following. The young boys gave evidence for the apprehension of Yatton and Davis, who appeared in court on the 28th. Both pleaded guilty to this and another charge of stealing from outside a shop – both were sentenced to three months' imprisonment with hard labour.

26 December 1887

On or about this date the unidentified, mutilated body of a woman was allegedly discovered near Commercial Road, Whitechapel. She was dubbed 'Fairy Fay' by Bruce Robertson in his 1948 article in *Reynolds News* (a name he obtained from the character of a dissolute woman mentioned in the popular song 'Polly Wolly Doodle All the Day'). It was stated in the accounts published in 1888 that she had been drinking most of the night in a pub in Mitre Square and was walking through the maze of alleys by Commercial Road after being turned out with everyone else when the pub closed, when her murderer struck. She was never formally identified and her murderer was never found. In truth 'Fairy Fay' never existed. Her murder was in fact only an accidental creation of the press, who, in the clamour to ascribe other murders to the 'Whitechapel Fiend' in September 1888, reported his 'previous crimes' and confused this alleged incident with the assault on Emma Smith (see 3 April, p. 60) and the serious attack on her fellow lodger, Margaret Hames, who was attacked in a similar place and nearby location on 8 December 1887 and wounded about the face and chest. She was released from the Whitechapel Infirmary two days after Boxing Day.

27 December 1888

The spirit of Christmas. Joseph South (25), a labourer of 7 Furze Street, Bromley, appeared at Thames Police Court charged with burglariously entering Thomas Bunn's grocer's shop on Box Street. He had been caught 'red handed' in the premises by Constable 501K and was taken into custody. When placed in the cell with Inspector Caleb Carter, South poured out his tragic tale: 'I sent my little girl for a Christmas Box last night and the old man would not give her one, so I thought I would help myself.'

28 December 1888

At Worship Street Court, Ellen Mahoney (39), described on the police sheet as 'an unfortunate' living in a common lodging house at 36 Flower and Dean Street, was charged with neglecting to provide necessary food and clothing for her infant child of 7 months and thereby endangering her life. Mary Price, the deputy of the lodging house, confirmed that Mahoney stayed there when she had the money. Price added that Mahoney had been in the habit of going out and leaving the child on a bench or table. The babe was 'always dirty' and in the opinion of the witness 'dying of starvation'. Price and another resident, Eliza Hildyard, attempted to feed the child, but Mahoney only abused those who tried to help. Fearing the dangerous condition the child was entering, Hildyard sent for a constable, who took it to Whitechapel Infirmary. On the statement of a doctor, the constable was sent to arrest the mother. In court she stated she did what she could for the child but she had no one to help support it. To ascertain fully the condition of the child, the prisoner was remanded for a week.

29 December 1888

Dr Danford Thomas held an inquest at Providence Hall, Edgware Road, into the death of Elizabeth Foakes (50), a housekeeper to a cab proprietor at Kilburn. Inspector Samuel Tilbrook of F Division stated he had been on duty in the Paddington Green police station the previous Monday morning when Foakes staggered in exclaiming, 'I have poisoned myself with oxalic acid.' A constable was sent for the divisional surgeon to procure an emetic but poor Elizabeth died before he arrived. Letters and some pawn tickets found on her person led to her identification, but quite why she had committed this act was not revealed. The jury simply returned a verdict of 'suicide when of unsound mind'.

30 December 1888

Julia Spickernell, 'a respectably dressed woman', appeared at Dalston Police Court charged with the murder of her daughter, Mabel Constance (8 or 9 months old). Inspector Scott of N Division and Mr Edward Spencer MRCS both attended the scene. The child was fully dressed and appeared to have been drowned. Spickernell was showing 'great mental emotion' and kept crying, 'I have done it; the Devil made me do it,' and exclaimed, 'Chop it up, chop it up' several times. At her trial she appeared subdued 'and did whatever she was told mechanically'. Dr Jackman diagnosed puerperal mania and expressed himself sure she was insane. Julia was removed to Holloway Prison in a cab, her stay to be 'until Her Majesty's pleasure be known'.

31 December 1888

The body of Montague John Druitt is recovered from the Thames. Born on 15 August 1857, Druitt graduated from New College, Oxford in 1880 and was soon teaching at a boy's boarding school in Blackheath. He added another string to his career when he studied law for the Bar and enjoyed steady employment in both fields. He was also an accomplished local level cricketer and member of the MCC. However, Druitt was soon dismissed from his position at the boarding school amid reports of 'serious trouble'. Could Druitt have been Jack the Ripper? Melville Macnaghten, Sir Charles Warren's replacement as Metropolitan Police Chief Constable was in no doubt. He named Druitt as his number one suspect in his memorandum (see 23 February, p. 38) where he points out that Druitt threw himself into the river seven weeks after the last murder and records, 'He was sexually insane and from private (information) I have little doubt but that his own family believed him to have been the murderer.'

Montague John Druitt.

ACKNOWLEDGEMENTS

It has been proved, yet again, that you meet some of the nicest people when researching the grimmest tales. I am privileged to count among my friends one of the leading Ripper authors, Stewart P. Evans, without whose singular generosity in sharing his extensive knowledge and archives with me this book would not have been possible or so enriched. I must also thank his wife Rosie for her kind and thoughtful hospitality.

In my travels researching this book it has been a pleasure to meet many helpful and interesting people, especially some real old 'East Enders'. There are sadly too many to mention all by name but I wish to record specific thanks to: James Nice, Dr Stephen Cherry, Jane Fall, Geoffrey Scott, Colin and Rachel Stonebridge, Larry and Doreen Golding (the Pearly King and Queen of Old Kent Road), Gordon Taylor, Archivist at the Salvation Army International Heritage Centre, The Museum of London, Tower Hamlets Local Studies Library, Whitechapel Library, University of East Anglia Library, The National Maritime Museum, Greenwich, The London Dungeon, The Galleries of Justice, Nottingham and the private police memorabilia and archive collections I have been given privileged access to. I also wish to record my respect for Donald Rumbelow whose book *The Complete Jack the Ripper* first kindled my interest in the Whitechapel Murders and their social context.

Sincere thanks, as ever, are due to Tony Smith from Shutters (Norwich) and Terry Burchell for his usual photographic wonders. Every attempt has been made to contact the owners of copyright for images used in this book. If any omission has been made it is not deliberate and no offence was intended.

Finally, but my no means least, I thank my family for their continuing love, support and forbearance of this temperamental author.

Note: All the pictures not specifically credited in the text are from the author's collection. The modern photographs of monuments and gravestones were taken by the author while on his travels in the public cemeteries of London over the last five years.